JESONIAN

JONATHAN RICHARD CRING

FIRST EDITION

LWS
BOOKS
©2007
www.lwsbooks.com

Also from Jonathan Richard Cring

FICTION:
I'M . . . the legend of the son of man
Liary
Mr. Kringle's Tales . . . 26 stories 'til Christmas
Holy Peace

NONFICTION:
Jesonian
Finding the Lily (to consider)
Digging for Gold (in the rule)
Preparing a Place (for myself)
20 Other Reasons to Kiss a Frog
Living a Legendary Life

SCREENPLAYS:

Hank's Place	Ought
Lenders Morgan	Bud
Baptism 666	The Man with the Red Hat
Gobel	(short)
Iz and Pal	Inside (short)
Newer	12/23 (short)

MUSICAL COMPOSITIONS:
I'M . . . a Jesonian serenade
Cloud of Witnesses (a requiem of renewal)
Have yourself a Clazzy little Christmas
To Everything a Season – Ingathering/Crystalline
To Everything a Season – Primavera/Soulstice
Opus 9/11
Symprophecy 2003
Jack
Symprophecy 2004
Being Human Symphony Live
Another Lily for You
The Kenilworth
Symprophecy 2005
Clazzy O – Let

LWS Books
P.O. Box 833
Hendersonville, TN 37077-0833
(800) 643-4718 ext. 74
lwsbooks.com

LWS Books are available at special quantity discounts for
bulk purchases for sales promotions, premiums, fund-
raising, and educational needs. Special books or book
excerpts also can be created to fit specific needs.
For details, write: LWS Books Special Markets,
P.O. Box 833, Hendersonville, TN 37077

ISBN 10: 0970436149
ISBN 13: 978-0-9704361-4-6

Library of Congress Control Number: 2006900003

For information on the author's touring schedule visit:
WWW.JANETHAN.COM

Cover Design by Angela Cring, Clazzy Studios

Manufactured and Printed in the United States

Table of Contents

Preface

Mike was a doctor *(insert vision of white coat, stethoscope, hospital room)* of psychology *(replace hospital room with patient laying on couch staring at ink blots)* for animals *(immediately conjure jungle scene—Tarzan walking with chimpanzee).* His specialty— dogs *(quickly inject vision of kennel, many barking hounds, man approaching with piece of meat in one hand and long needle in the other).* In particular, poodles *(change scene from kennel to patio next to pool, foo foo dog held by socialite woman and doctor in khaki slacks taking notes).* Poodles who have been traumatized *(imagine fu-fu dog with flattened fur and furrowed brow weeping into golden dog dish).* The source of their trauma being that their fur has been dyed pink *(now we have a problem. make the scene Paris café, everyone wearing berets, including the pink poodle, the doctor of dog poodle psychology sipping wine, petting pink fur reassuringly)* ,which has caused them to develop a strong emotionally-based halitosis *(please see doctor with beret offering sad-eyed mutt a breath mint).* Which causes their owners to alienate them *(interject socialite lady with a clothespin on her nose turning her head, looking in a catalogue to purchase a less fragrant breed).* So the poodle has taken on the attributes of a German shepherd *(remove beret, insert German war helmet with spike on top, dog chewing on bratwurs).* And since he is a French poodle who believes he is a German shepherd *(maintain image of dog, inlay french fries instead of bratwurst)* and since the French and German people are natural enemies *(hmmm ... how about a photo of a bratwurst and a french fry fighting?),* the dog spends his whole day chasing his own tail to bite his own butt. The end.

As you can see, stopping the story at any given moment because we might think we understand all the necessary details can leave us in quite a visual tizzy.

Jesus was the son of God, *(interject images of flying Christ surrounded by angels and doves)* the savior of the world, *(think about reflections of cross, nails, blood, crown of thorns and weeping women)* born in a manger *(that one's easy — shepherds, wise men, sheep, donkeys, and beatific Mary and Joseph).* Spent his formative years in Egypt, *(wow — that's a tough one — uh, maybe Joseph working on the Pyramids as the little boy wearing the Egyptian hat plays in the sand turning snakes into rabbits)* was rejected by his family, *(produce image of hostile talk show live from Nazareth with brothers and sisters arguing but still beatific)* enjoyed the company of children *(please immediately repress image of Catholic priest; interweave Jesus in cardigan-type robe, slippers, and Mr. Roger's neighborhood with palm trees)* but also liked to party at the home of well-known sinners *(wow, this is getting tough. How do you blend Gandhi with Al Capone? How about creating image of Jesus turning over poker tables?),* So much so that people said that he was their friend *(Jesus picking up poker table and chips, apologizing for temper tantrum)*. Religious people did not like him *(introduce character of Sunday School teacher frowning and smacking Jesus' hand with a ruler)*. They even plotted against him *(fade in to scene of church board meeting with pastor removing gold star from Jesus' attendance record)*. They decided to kill him *(this one has me stumped — plant scene of choir director gunning down off-pitch tenor)* because he refused to hate Rome *(wriggle out a memory of the Ben Hur guy who lost the chariot race sharing a nice roast beef sandwich with Jesus)* and he taught people to take personal responsibility for their lives instead of blaming God and the politics of the day *(No image available — who **does** that?)*. And did I mention he also claimed to be the son of God? *(Somehow the angel and dove thing doesn't quite fit anymore.)*

Obviously, there is always more to the story. I guess that's what this book is all about—the man and his message, and how it has gotten lost with men massaging the egos of overly pious parties. Come and join me on the journey.

(***Jesonian*** is based on Luke 7:31-35)

Sitting One
Likening

A pair of bulls walk into a china shop. One turns to the other and says, "You go right and I'll go left and we'll meet at the back door."

A pair of bulls, sitting down at a delicious dinner. One bull says to the other, "I don't know how it got started. All I know is that I told the National Enquirer, I was well-**read**."

A pair of bulls, spending some time out in the pasture. One turns to the other and says, "What I wouldn't give for a nice, thick, juicy cow."

Which is not to be confused with a **parable**, which is a story told using common terms to convey a message. I'm sure Webster could have defined it much better, but I couldn't find my dictionary— probably holding up the end of a bed somewhere.

There seems to be a great fear to compare. I think it probably began with the madcap apples and oranges mis- understanding. You know the one I mean: "It's like comparing apples and

11

oranges." Actually, they compare rather nicely. Both are fruit. Both have seeds on the inside. Both have Vitamin C, both have fiber and both keep the doctor away. The only obvious difference is their color. Speaking of that, I recently asked a group of teenagers what color an apple was. They became vehement and angry when I told them that red, green and yellow were incorrect, for only about ten per cent of an apple is its skin hue. The rest of the apple is white. So can we compare apples and oranges? More easily than we thought.

A carpenter from Nazareth named Jesus came along and chose to illustrate his doctrine by using stories. Interestingly, most of his stories dealt with farming, fishing, fatherhood, sonship, servants, job quality, and banquets. He really doesn't tell a specific parable about carpentry. Certainly seems he was quite glad to have left the shop.

Still, he chose to speak in story form to convey his ideas—ideas which now have digressed to being proclaimed from the throats of stuffed-collared theo- logians.

"A certain man went forth; a certain man had two sons; the kingdom of heaven is like; two men built a house; there were ten virgins (by the way, five of them were foolish) . . ." In instance after instance, Jesus contends that the best way to propel a message is comparison, or to **liken** it unto to something else. It just begs me to ask the question—why? I mean, if you have come from heaven with this very specific mission, and you know you're on a ticking clock towards your own death, and you have great hopes that your words will survive your own assassination, why would you gamble the shining principles of your philosophy to be interpreted by poor, Bedouin laymen? Why tell stories when there are religionists all around you who analyze every jot and tittle of Mosaic Law to find the subtle nuance of translation which will foster their favorite interpretation?

This is exactly the question that the disciples asked him. "Why don't you speak plainly, man?" His answer was simple—just like his parables—and two-fold:

1. *The people are dull to hearing.* Folks were inundated with information from both rabbi and Rome—tiny, subtle nuances of Jewish law and large paragraphs of Roman edict thrust before them daily. Their ears were deafened by meaningless conversation. Jesus selected not to be

just another voice crying in the wilderness, punctuating his themes with the normal jargon or mystical vernacular of the religionists.

2. ***It is not given for the common man to know the secrets of the Kingdom.*** If you isolate that statement, it reeks a bit of elitism, which most authors would rationalize away as being misinterpreted. I don't think we misunderstand him. I think if you're beginning a movement with fishermen, tax collectors, whores and prostitutes, it doesn't hurt your cause to make them feel they are given a special position — a personal audience with truth. Is it elitism if the people are not informed that they are being left out of deeper meaning? Or is it mercy when you don't force deeper meaning on people who are still drowning in the last deluge of church teaching?

We do know this — that when Jesus got alone with his disciples he explained to them what each and every story meant. But I also guarantee you, he anticipated that those people left out of the inner sanctum of explanations would go off and share the stories with each other in the pursuit of finding hidden translation, and therefore keep the messages alive for hours, perhaps days, longer than the average rabbi's discourse.

Of course, you live by the parable, you may end up dying by the parable, because it was one of his tales about destroying the temple and building it back in three days that they used at his trial to prove that he was a seditionist. Tough crowd.

What is it we hate about comparison? I never met a woman who liked to be compared to another woman. Can you imagine that? "No, honey, what I meant was, she has bigger breasts than you, but you have a prettier face . . ." These are the famous last words of the solitary man. We don't want to compare our children, even though some natural competition exists in life itself. After all, an A student is not a C student. But even in our schools we're trying to eliminate any semblance of contest, out of fear of discouraging those who do not fare well by comparison.

So where does this take us? I believe we have created an *emotional communism* — we all are supposed to feel the same way so no one will feel better and make others feel worse. So those who are destined to excel are corralled into a

limiting horse sense which bridles them
to coexist with those who may be destined
to be saddled up for service. The words
seem harsh to us — "leader," "excellence"
and "service" — seemingly diametrically
opposed. Yet in another parable, Jesus
tells us, "He that would be master
(excellent) must be servant of all
(service)." There is the balance. The road
to mastery, which is what we should be
pursuing, is in learning how to service our
fellow man so that what we do and think
is not just theory, but becomes a visual
articulation to be displayed before all
men. But too often we pretend that
leaders just naturally rise to the top.

Unless there is competition and
comparison, nothing will rise to the top
unless it is backed or pushed upward
through promotion. Nature itself tells us
exactly how things should work. If we
would just study our planet, and stop
believing that we are so superior to the
birds, bees and cattle, we would begin to
understand the unction that God placed
into the natural order to create a function
for our lives. For instance, a bird who
does not build a nest is not awarded a
certificate of participation. A cow who
does not produce milk is not determined
to be "one of the winners." And a bee who

doesn't do his part buzzing the hive is not considered to be "part of the team." In like manner, neither are we happy as people when we do not find full disclosure of our gifts, or when we are not motivated by friends and enemies alike to achieve our full package of detailed success.

Likening. We need comparison. If God came and explained the cosmos, He would probably sit down and say, "You know it's kind of like this." Or, "How many of you ever ate a hot dog?" Common words create common understanding. Yet, in the pursuit of individuality, we have tried to make each man uncommon to the other. Although we know this to be a farce, we perpetuate the myth of our own uniqueness, when the truth of the matter is, the sameness of our beings in spirit and the desires of our hearts are what make us brothers and sisters.

Jesus had a particularly bad day. The religious leaders had gotten on his nerves, the disciples had hatched an unusually dumb scheme, and even his morning dates had a bitter aftertaste. He speaks to those in earshot and he says, "Whereunto shall I liken?"

Perhaps you should admire someone who waxes poetic when

17

confronted with idiocy instead of lashing out with the profanity *du jour*. He decides to keep his sense of humor by comparing. I'm so glad he did. Because if Jesus had ever decided to get on a jag of honesty, no ego would have survived. **Likening**: the decision to compare in the hopes of allowing the cream of truth to rise to the top

"Whereunto shall I liken?" Liken what? Well, that would be our next sitting, wouldn't it?

Sitting Two
The Men of this Generation

Religion is always easy to identify. First, a set of rules — usually spoken by flesh and engraved in stone. Secondly, those rules are almost always targeted at children and women — what they can't or shouldn't do. Quite frankly, religion just does not like women and children, concluding that, "Children should be seen and not heard" and "women should be not obscene but silly and absurd."

Why is it that when religion becomes fundamental in practice, it targets women and children as the bag and baggage of all problems? When men are in charge of theology, they don't lust, women dress inappropriately; men aren't bad fathers, children are rebellious. So therefore, spank them, taunt them, ridicule them, criticize them — these two great creations, the last and most phenomenal of God's miracles, become the victim of every religious edict and marauding minister who is looking for a cause to explain all the "sin in the camp." Please comprehend this—man was not the last human creation — woman followed him. She was certainly an improvement. Don't you think God would enhance his second effort? But He didn't stop there. Deep within the DNA of man and woman lay the masterful perfection of a human child, the last and greatest hatching of the Almighty. Thus Jesus says, "Unless we become as little children we will not enter the kingdom of God." So I am a man, trying to ascend through woman to reach my human destination as a child of innocence.

So when Jesus starts his parable on "likening," he says "I'm going to talk about the men of this generation." It would have been much more popular for him to speak against women and children and to use them as the buffer of his insights, considering that this little story was probably delivered in front of a testosterone-driven audience. Certainly, receptivity would have been guaranteed if he would have begun his discourse with "Let me talk to you about the women . . . not to mention those bratty kids . . . " He certainly would have been guaranteed chuckles just with his opening line rather than the grumbling which occurred when he chose to target — the men.

What could possibly cause Jesus to think that men could be lumped into a generation? Are we not innately unique? Are we not singularly purposed? Are we

not islands of passion unto ourselves?
(Please let me stop here before I start to
giggle . . .)

No. Actually, we have a spirit that
aspires to attain an isolated and
motivated life, but we normally look
around us and imitate the closest fellow to
us, partially out of fear of rejection, but
mostly out of convenience.

Ah, yes. Convenience. More than
just a store. Convening. Clumping.
Collecting, herding. Joining and meshing
our thinking into the thinking of others
until it is so crushed by the sheer weight
of opinion that nothing of individuality or
originality can survive. Yes. All creativity
is suffocated under the press of the horde.
We become men, caught up in a
generational hamburger patty, pressed
together, pushed down, grilled up and
served. Do we dare disagree?

Unfortunately, in this kind of social
meat-grinder, contention can bring
disfavor, which will cause us to be
eyeballed carefully by those who are more
in step with the thinking of the clan. So
what can we do?

Because often we are unable to
express our personal sense in words or
ideas, we take all of our energies and try
to display our freedom through material

preferences. "Bill likes a Ford, but I prefer a Chevy." "Sam takes mustard on his hot dog, but not me. I prefer kraut." "Mike likes the wide screen, but for me there's nothing like thirty-six inches."

In the scheme of things, little meaningless choices seem to carry the weight and the burden of our whole conscious effort to be different. And even then we have to be cautious — careful to avoid the pinks and polka dots or anything that might deter from the macho image that makes us "men" rather than being cast into the pit of oblivion with the women and children, who labor under a religious system while the men herd with the bulls trying to gain distinction through their material choices.

"Whereunto shall I liken the men of this generation?"

Well, Jesus, I don't know about your day, but I do understand how men are made today. You just have to watch three hours of prime-time television with commercials! The sitcoms, dramas and advertisements make it clear what their selected profile should be if they want to be part of the flow of the masculine tide.

1. Men are stronger, but generally dumber than women, but in the long run, stronger is better.
2. Men are from Mars, and women are from Venus, with no possibility of gaining enough humanity to find common ground.
3. Men want sex, and women want to shop. A deal must be struck.
4. After men bungle the parenting situation, women come in and soothe the hurt feelings so that the man, of good conscience, can go out and make more money.
5. Any woman can be wooed. The more superficially it's done, the better.
6. Men bond over sports and a communion table consisting of the cup of beer and the wafer of pepperoni pizza.
7. Men are opinionated, which makes them cute.
8. Women can be strong, but eventually are weakened by trial and circumstance and are in need of a shoulder to cry on.
9. Children are always trouble and rebellious — never want to share their feelings. It is not that men are inaccessible — rather, all children are

teenagers, therefore all children are mixed-up disciplinary problems.

10. Men listen to women and become sensitive only to achieve sexual pleasure. When they want to fellowship or think, they hang around other men, thus creating a cult of *homo-emoters*, lamenting their failure with the women as they discuss the subtleties of the remote control.

It is a frightening list. Certainly makes you nervous that in our present political climate, there is a hairy hand on every red button controlling the nuclear weapons. Jesus pulls no punches. He does not condone a male dominated society. But if men are going to insist on dominating, then men must begin to take responsibility for the conclusions, instead of acting like they are the innocent bystanders in a one-act play. "The men of this generation" — what will Jesus tell us about them? And what will we learn about their individuality versus mob mentality?

Well, he starts off with an interesting simile. You see, he says, "Whereunto shall I liken the men of this generation? Well, they are like . . ."

Sitting Three
Children in the Marketplace

It must happen around age twelve or thirteen. We reach a certain size, or we sprout a particular vehement attitude that not only makes us difficult to correct, but produces a physical intimidation level that our parents no longer want to deal with. We have become "too much to handle." We are "too big to spank." We have become . . . *incorrigible.* We are so self-possessed that our parents, who once received our hugs, now receive nothing but cold shoulders. Perhaps the parents should step in and say, "Listen, you little twerp, I don't care how big you think you are, or how smart you think you are, there still is a helluva lot you've got to learn, so sit down and shut up or you will spend the next two weeks drinking your pizza through a straw."

No! We can't say that. It is gruesome to our sensitivity. It is foul and condemning. It would taint their self-image. So, we do a lot of sighing. I don't know how we learned to sigh so well — I guess we saw our parents and retained the image for later use. But sighing is what teenagers seek, the aspiration of all their efforts. An exasperated parent is eventually an acquiescent one. A parent who will not scream back his objection to behavior problems will eventually give in to nasty attitudes in order to "just have some peace and quiet." Teenagers count on this! They live for the moment when Mom and Dad say, "Well, I don't want to fight about this." They smile, restraining a chortle. They've won. Their ridiculous habit will go unchecked because the parents fear confrontation, or worse, are terrified of becoming "overwrought" and "the bad guy."

Because of this, all the elements of style, class and grace that we needed to learn stopped at thirteen, and unfortunately, are gradually eroded away as the young buck or the flittering deer go out to make their own way, free of correction and devoid of instruction.

Now here comes the phenomenon. Jesus makes it perfectly clear. These young folk pass through the years of adolescence; their bodies and genitalia growing to full adult size, but their toleration, fortitude and emotional reactions still remain at a thirteen-year-old level. So they are thrust into the marketplace of life and the workaday world with bodies representative of their actual age, minds educated to their saturation point, but souls empty of experiential spirituality and an emotional make-up stuck at thirteen.

They are children in the marketplace.

They are well trained, they are well groomed, but they are ill prepared to deal with the ebb and flow of normal life. So, like a thirteen-year-old, if they act disgusted enough, or frustrated enough, or really disappointed enough, they expect someone to give in and give them their way.

When I was eighteen, I went on a quest in search of an adult. Candidly, I knew I myself was not one. Now, having crossed a half-century of life, I still have not found one — and too terrified to look in the mirror. Bluntly, nobody told us we had to grow up! Nobody told us that time and chance happens to all! Nobody made it clear that it rains on the just and the unjust! Nobody gave us a grade in "karma — what goes around comes around."

So frozen at the emotional age of thirteen, we pout. People often wonder why there are so many divorces in this country. My God, it's simple! After you've been married for more than four years, no mate is going to let you have your way anymore simply because you stump and stomp. Because they won't give in to your grumbling, they naturally lose some of their appeal to you. You don't understand . . . you were able to manipulate your parents — why not your husband or wife? And predictably, here come the words: "She doesn't understand me." Or, "he is such a slob and a chauvinist." So begins the quest to find a new lover who is so desperate for personal attention that he or she will temporarily grant us our childish quirks. Our quirks salved, we become convinced that we no longer love that former sexual partner who now has become merely a challenger to our childish whims.

Or how about this? Get on the freeway any Monday through Friday. Look around you. Need to change lanes? I do believe that's two weeks notice. Want to drive the speed limit? It is recommended that you park and take the bus. Looking for a little courtesy and a friendly wave? Go to Disneyland. You must learn the profile of the day — cell phone in hand, ego intact, steering wheel clutched, foot to the floor — "this is my road."

Children in the marketplace. We have tossed the keys to twenty-thousand dollar weapons into the hands of people who have not been questioned since the last time their parents asked them to clean their room. Some people are afraid of terrorists. I, for one, deathly fear . . . traffic. Traffic with cars driven by children, who physically can see over the steering wheel but emotionally can see no one but themselves.

Where are the grown-ups? Where are the people who suffer defeat with grace? Where are the mature souls with a word of wisdom in the time of crisis instead of a deceptive plan to avoid discovery? Where are the leaders who show us their pimples instead of sinisterly covering up their blemishes? I personally do not care what mistakes people make. I do not thirst for a perfect man, woman or child. I hunger to be at the banquet table with human souls who are emotionally mature enough to face up to their inadequacies, survive a set back, truthfully assess their pros and cons, and proceed with perseverance, to play another day.

"Whereunto shall I liken the men of this generation? They are children in the marketplace." Don't get me wrong — I

like children. I don't like childish.
Sometimes I can even tolerate childish, as
long as a child is not in charge of me.
Maybe I can even put up with them being
in charge of me, if they don't control the
life and death of other fellow travelers.

But they do.

Nations don't war with each other.
Try as I may to understand, I have never
seen two borders have a conflict. I have
never seen landmasses spew lava at each
other, exploding in fiery heaps of
destruction. I have really never seen
religions launch crusades against infidels.
Frightening, isn't it? It all boils down to
"Bill doesn't like Bob." Or perhaps better
stated, "Jack doesn't like Ahib." And God
knows, if they don't like each other,
compromise is impossible. I guess the
thought is, if I didn't have to compromise
with my parents, and they controlled my
allowance, why would I even think about
negotiating with you? Especially when I
can so easily destroy you.

And while we're on the subject,
please don't ask me anymore if I want
fries with that, when you are so oblivious
to your job that you forget to put my
milkshake in the sack. Please don't tell
me I'm in good hands in your company,
when you use the uncertain state of our

world affairs to gouge me with insurance premiums. Please don't tell me you're the friendly grocery store and then hassle me because I want to return a gallon of sour milk. Perhaps I have digressed.

But still, someone lied to us. They told us that sprouting hair and sporting a diploma guaranteed us a place in the adult world. They forgot to mention that we needed to emotionally mature — learning to survive disappointment and muster a fresh, daily effort.

Can you see Jesus' point? He was dealing with religious leaders who should have had the sense to know that religion, by its very nature, was not created to please God, but rather, initiated by God to please men and teach them to peacefully coexist with each other, and emotionally mature in order to negotiate the twists and the turns of the natural order. Can you see how frustrating it must have been to this practical teacher, Jesus, to see hungry people, Jewish people, begging alms from their Roman captors, as their religious leaders walked the streets carrying plans for a new addition to the golden temple? Can you see how this young Nazarene was infuriated with an excuse-driven society that relegated women and children to the status of livestock, while insisting the hour of prayer be honored, of course, religiously?

Are we different today? Maybe we have better dental hygiene than the average Jewish man walking the streets in Jesus' day. Maybe our underarms smell of menthol and lilac instead of grain and sweat, but at the heart of the matter, beating in the breast of every man is a childish tyrant who too soon was granted his way by parents too intimidated to disagree.

Does it take a toll? Answer the question yourself. Are young men dying on battlefields? Is this their will or the actions of children in the marketplace? Are babies dying of starvation? Is this their choice or the callous oversight of children in the marketplace? Are inferior products being released into society, often with dangerous conclusions? Is this the consumer's preference or cost cuts in production from children in the marketplace?

We can make a difference. But it will take more than ribbons on our lapels and flags waving in the wind. It will take each and every one of us admitting that we don't always know what is best — even for ourselves — and that we are in the learning process of a planet ancient to our years, and often beyond our comprehension. We are in need of input. We can no longer afford the luxury of seclusion. We must begin to accept the fact, not only that each man is my brother, but that each man, in some way, is my teacher. For, after all, childishness ceases when the child agrees to listen. Do not settle for leaders, either secular or spiritual, who thrust a sword in the ground and insist that their way is the only way. Even when our spiritual doctrines seem black and white, we ourselves need to remain open with shades of gray. Is this heresy or weakness? I think the true weakness is anyone who thinks that by producing a daily crop of stubborn behavior, that success, personal contentment, and peace can be harvested.

Children in the marketplace . . . now wait a minute. If they're children in the marketplace, it means they are probably not meant to be there. And if they're not meant to be there, what makes us think they would be comfortable in their own skin? So guess what? These children are . . . just sitting around.

Sitting Four
Sitting

It was the Christmas of my son Jerrod's eighth year, and he was strongly urging us to purchase a particular toy which, of course, was the most popular and most demanded present of the year. After an exhaustive quest, making Hercules look like a lethargic whiner, we found the prize, wrapped it, delivered it under the tree, and sat by anxiously awaiting Christmas morning . . . and oh, what a payoff for our hours of searching! His eyes lit up; he released a tiny screech, and boy, toy and Dad interlocked in a glorious embrace. It was terrific. I felt so good. To be able to fulfill the dream of my young son and provide the essence of his desire was an emotional intoxicant.

About two hours later, still drunken with glee and self-admiration, I walked into the room to discover my young son sitting in a chair, droopy-shouldered, pouty-lipped, with melancholy eyes.

"What's wrong?" I asked, assuming terminal illness.

"I'm bored," he replied, elongating the word to four syllables — the depth of his despair.

I'm not proud of this, but at that moment, I wished to kill him. I know it sounds extreme, but flash backs of pushing and shoving through department stores, parking kilometers from front doors of shopping malls, and aching feet which still throbbed, temporarily took over my sensibility and feelings of fatherhood.

This bored child must die — an audacious ant and bumbling brat who must be curtailed for the crime of his dastardly denseness — eradicated. Of course, I didn't. He is married and has given us a grandchild, which kind of makes up for it.

Children are naturally active. We spend most of our time trying to calm them down. They bounce around the room, often off the walls, only landing in a heap when they are either exhausted or *bored*. Is there anything worse than coming across a child who is so bored that he is *sitting*?

For you see, once the children get into the marketplace, and realize that they are out of their league and life is not the bowl of cherries once promised; once they realize that they will not own the company but the company extracts hours of labor from them for a predetermined menial salary, then they quickly become bored with their lives and their jobs.

Boredom. Here's how it works. To cover our egomaniacal obsession with entertainment, we have justified boredom as a viable, human experience. Of course, nothing could be further from the truth. Basically, when all the smoke clears from cynical rhetoric, and all the naysayers have weighed in, human beings function best in an atmosphere of **excitement** and **happiness**.

In our society we propagate the notorious notion that introverts are a natural phenomenon — still waters that run deep, even though nature tells us that any water that is not free-flowing is rancorous, stale and poison. Yes — there it is. Boredom is the poison to the human soul that infects our whole being with the malignancy of self-pity. Children don't sit unless they're exhausted, bored or exhaustively bored.

It is an unholy ruse: we encourage the quiet soul, the contemplative discerner when we know deep in our hearts that we are possibly condemning this person to a life of loneliness, desperation and despair. For every one

36

individual who is naturally reclusive, yet productive, there are a thousand people who have retired into their shell because they have ceased to believe in the potential of joy, the reality of abundant living, and opt to become the bored and the lost "silent majority."

The *true* natural state? Children are meant to be happy. Children were designed to be excited. Yet our children in the marketplace are not prepared for the competition, the hunt, the perpetual hassle, and the occasional fit of desperation. So when the sheer stark reality of existence comes to play, there is no reservoir of energy and faith to draw from their beings to eliminate the human horror of boredom.

Why is boredom so bad? Doesn't everybody get bored? All boredom is rooted in the belief that I, as a human being, need to be entertained, not that I, as a human being, need to exude and produce entertainment. Therefore creativity is out of the question, thinking is exhausting, and sensitivity only makes the boredom more pronounced.

Boredom also induces the fallacious conclusion of accidental sin — the ***BPS factor: boredom-produced sin.*** For after all, is it plausible for an excited, active young person with a great self-image and a general state of happiness to be lured into a life of drug addiction? Do jubilant beings self-destruct? Can happiness occupy the same space as boredom? There's the word: *happiness*. We live in a space of time when the children in the marketplace, who are sitting because they're bored, have become cynical toward the concept of happiness. For the sarcastic, to be happy is to be naïve. In the thinking of the bored man, happiness means oblivion to the true angst of life. We are pummeled with the concept that happiness is, at best, a temporary affair.

Yet we have this teacher named Jesus, who, in the prelude of his major manifesto, the Sermon on the Mount, makes happiness the goal of every situation, even those scenarios that might seem to be less than joyous occasions, i.e., poor in spirit, mourners, persecuted for righteousness sake, the meek, and the action of mercy. He proposes that a blessed life, a happy life, is the bottom line for evaluating our human status. In another discourse he tells his followers that he has come to the planet that our joy might be full. In still another, that we might have life, and it more abundantly.

He says, "In the world you have tribulation, but be of good cheer — I have overcome the world." Even one night, when he's in a boat and a storm arises, and his disciples, in a flurry of apprehension, awaken him to address their plight of death, he tells them to be of good cheer.

What was he thinking? Isn't this insensitive? How can I yuk it up when I'm about to go down? What is the underlying message? So, we're about to drown, and you want us to laugh because we'll have our mouths open, the water will come in and we'll die more quickly?

Or is good cheer the only way to remain calm in a crisis, and is calm what is necessary for great decision-making? For does desperation brought on by boredom with life and fear of circumstances make us more likely to crumble under the pressure and more susceptible to the lottery of failure — dashing all of our hope? (By the way, they didn't drown.)

Once the children are thrust into a marketplace where they are not prepared to cope with the everyday disappointments and the languishing hours of what may seem to be meaningless labor, they soon sit down on the job. Yes, you've heard that phrase — "he's sitting down on the job!"

He's bored.

Back for a moment to this BPS. How does it affect our lives? The children in the marketplace who are sitting because they're bored soon succumb to temptations brought on by a feeling of being cheated. Thus the bored businessman, feeling cheated by life, embezzles from his company. The bored housewife, feeling deprived of affection, relents to the affair. The bored teenager, unable to compete with his peers, debilitates in a haze of smoke and drugs. The bored minister finds solace in the adoring church secretary. The bored teacher allows herself to cut corners and not provide adequate education to her students. The bored air-traffic controller misses a blip on the screen, and the bored priest, feeling shackled by the rigors of celibacy, victimizes young lads. Are they guiltless? No, they are childish and bored.

Sitting. When you get right down to it, sitting is not really resting. Rather, it is that "no man's land" between lying down and getting up and going — a perch of indecision. It is often a seat of discomfort due to feelings of inadequacy, fear, and apprehension. So the young man sits in front of the video games when a more exciting, happy choice would be to pursue the young lady of his dreams. The frustrated factory worker sits in front of the television set when the more exciting, happy choice would be to finish that book of poems or work on that car he was trying to rebuild.

Children in the marketplace, feeling inadequate, feeling incomplete to the task, soon despair of trying and become sitting ducks for all sorts of self-piteous temptation and self-loathing behavior.

How can we know if our childishness has caused us to become candidates for boredom or even BPS? Ask yourself some questions:

1. What is the last thing I did in my life that was born in my heart, nurtured in my brain and acted out as a creative notion of my own?
2. How often do I watch through a second show on television that I don't really enjoy simply because I'm waiting for bedtime?
3. When was the last time I had a conversation with another human being that didn't include at least

one session of complaining about my situation?

4. How often do I allow myself to become depressed, not because of circumstance, but because I am sad because I don't know exactly what to do?

5. How long has it been since I have studied something to improve my understanding instead of giving up because I don't understand?

6. How many times have I sat in a religious service and had my mind wander because what was being said seemed irrelevant, but I really had no courage to quibble over the material?

7. How many times do I complain about the hassles in my life when I know that without hassle I cannot change my situation and improve my lot?

8. How many friends do I have who I allow to challenge and question me to keep me sharp instead of agreeing with me and reassuring me that I'm just fine the way I am?

9. How often am I tempted to do something wrong because there's just not enough right going on? And finally,

10. Do I ever go to sleep because I
    don't know what else to do?

Jesus makes it clear that he likened
the men in his generation to children in
the marketplace, people who were thrust
into the quagmire of existence before they
were emotionally prepared to handle the
competition and change in climate, so
they quickly find themselves sitting,
watching the parade go by, totally bored.

Remember, we sit to observe; we
stand to act. So as you become an
observer, observation by its very nature
produces a haughtiness lending itself to
criticism. The sad summary: if my life is
not exciting, and I'm not really happy,
how dare you be excited and happy in my
midst? Therefore, it becomes important
to stop the spread of glee, essential to
disprove the value of enthusiasm.

To safeguard our soul from too
much self-examination, it becomes
necessary for us to clique, to form unholy
alliances of childish and bored market-
placers. After all, when you're bored,
happiness just makes you feel sad, and
excitement just seems too exhausting. So,
in this way, joy is the enemy of all who sit
to criticize.

The squeeze begins — pressured on one side to fall into transgression and personal frailties, and challenged on the other to stop being bored and find a state of happiness. To escape the pressure, we must surround ourselves with enough fellow-bored-souls, coagulating together into a great clot of critical complaining to secure us from being penetrated by the piercing potential of an exciting, happy life.

Sitting Five
Calling One to Another

Religion might just work if it weren't organized. Patriotism might be a quaint sentiment if it didn't degenerate into nationalism. Whenever more than three people print a pamphlet, sew a flag, sign a decree, develop a pledge card, generate a roster, foster a team or promise an allegiance, the end result is always the repression of diversity.

Don't get me wrong — I believe we need fellowship, but my soul shudders at the reasons and motivations for clumping into bodies of belief. For as soon as people discover that their childish ways will not bring success in the marketplace, and a kind of snooty, angry boredom settles into their souls about their destiny, they begin to search for other malcontents who agree with their conclusions. They begin "calling one to another."

Oh, it can seem quite harmless. Just in a passing conversation at a local grocery store: "Kind of hot today, don't you think?" Just try answering, "Yeah, but I kind of like it." It is a great conversation killer. Even this little, seemingly innocent question is often a query, a verbal test, if you will, to find out if you are amongst the ranks of the ill-prepared, and therefore, the bored masses. No, for some reason, we have been taught to link. We seem to be on a mission to bond with others. It seems noble, almost spiritual. If we were joining with others to create a fellowship of mature, growing beings, it would be enriching. But too often the reasons for melding are not noble at all.

Any fellowship should have three purposes for existing: (1) To nurture diversity (2) to celebrate needful change, and (3) to instigate excitement and happiness.

Honestly, any gathering of human beings that does not accentuate these three virtuous pursuits is basically what we might call a cult of the *"gosh darns."* I call them the "gosh-darns" because, out of political correctness, they are not quite willing to damn it all, but they are certainly dissatisfied with the general complexion of how life is spinning so far. These "gosh darns" develop a criteria for membership, which is also three-fold: (1) Because life is such a serious endeavor, we must use caution at all times; (2) there are many paths and actions which need to be avoided to keep us from falling into disfavor with our higher consciousness, be it God, the president or one's own moral code; (3) though we tolerate others, we commune most frequently with those of like, precious paranoia.

Jesus, in his teachings, called hell Gehenna. Well, Gehenna was the garbage dump of the Jerusalem community, where all the wasted, discarded, useless, putrid and unnecessary trash found a disposal site to decompose together. Thus hell does not exist so much as a lake of fire as it does as a toxic dump for the human soul. So what causes us to be carted away? The dump awaits those who have given up on the power that is supposed to occur as a natural evolution in our everyday thinking and feeling. Instead, these bored individuals believe that things should remain the same and consequently, they seep into clumps of people who celebrate the past – a past when seemingly there were no problems for the human traveler. It becomes the old, incompetent dirge: "Let's go back-wards to go forward"

So in a church situation, the liturgy often reeks of self-incrimination — in essence: "Lord, look at me, this poor sinner who cannot learn your ways"— which at first might appear to the unschooled ear to be humility, but really is a resignation to the sadness of life and the inability of us as humans to excel and "be perfect even as our Father in heaven is perfect,"— once again, Jesus, from his "big talk on the hill."

Calling one to another. You just have to smile at the idea that Jesus, who lived when there were no telephones, e-mails or video communication, leaps through time to say that these people are "calling one to another." After all, how many phone conversations digress into a bevy of excuses and complaints? Truthfully, if happiness and excitement were our pursuit and fellowship of diversity was our goal, we would talk less, enjoy each other more, and celebrate our prolific, industrious lives. Instead, we accumulate in groups to discuss our boredom and continue that ritual until we are even more bored than when we arrived.

I often watch with wonder on television when they videotape a meeting of a church, city council or even our Congress. Within moments, the monotone of subdued, lethargic transpirings place me in a mental stupor.

Fresh thinking and innovative ideas are repressed by droning, depressive, repetitive rhetoric.

It makes you want to ask, why don't we want to be happy? Is excitement so bad? Why must we find others who forecast gloom and agree with our inclement thinking? Why must we collect into denominations and organizations fostering childish boredom? Why must we create a language for the "gosh-darns," permeated with the illusion that there is someplace better than where we presently are?

Do we understand why Jesus landed on earth? It certainly wasn't to prove he was God. If God wanted to be God, he was already God. God needed to do nothing else to remain God. God had his God thing down. God was a God and was doing God well.

So why was there a need for a New Testament, a revolution in spirituality? Because God wasn't doing the *human* thing well. He was like a great car manufacturer without a parts supply house. He knew exactly how to make people but had failed to find a way to deliver us from the evil that so easily beset us. Distance had created a chasm of misunderstanding. We no longer loved

49

God; we only feared him when a moment's reflection of mortality startled our sensibilities. Godless, loveless and hopeless, we had collected ourselves into disgruntled cults of lamentation.

"Are you as miserable as I am?" Even in our hymns, in our prayers, there is still often the underlying message of "Isn't life a bitch?" We are dissatisfied customers. Certainly it must occur to us that a God who failed to create a planet filled with excitement and happiness may be just as inept at building an eternal life teeming with adventure? If God is incapable of finding a way for his will to be done on earth, how insipid might his Heaven experiment be? No wonder people say "God damn it" so much — because they certainly do not believe in their hearts that he can bless it.

Once we decide that our childish ways of dealing with disappointment do not promote us in this world but rather stagnate us into a puddle of self-piteous putty, we, as naturally gregarious beings, still need to find those souls who agree with our dismal conclusion. What does the bumper sticker say? "Life sucks and then you die." The only thing missing from that is a resounding *Amen*.

What will break this hideous spell on mankind — this dark cloud of gloom? It will take a spirited anarchy and each of us being willing to release our tenacious hold on tradition, or should I call it "tread"-ition? A relentless march to a depressing doom. It will also take people unafraid of temporarily being alienated from public opinion.

I remember one day I suggested to a group of men in a barber shop that we all might be happier in our everyday lives if we just sat down at the breakfast table with our wives and waited for conversation to stimulate an idea of what to do in the day. In other words, talk to the person you say you love until a new idea comes up that you would both like to tackle and accomplish. Well, the response was fascinating. First, a nervous giggle. Then a series of passing glances to each other to conjointly confirm my insanity. A couple of cleared throats, an attempt at a joke, and then someone quickly changed the subject. Undaunted and unwilling to be ignored, I had the audacity to pose the question again. This time, the conver-sational topic was changed with a bit of gruffness and a slight warning that I should drop it or face recrimination — of course, in the most civilized way possible

— by being ignored. How simple it is to make people mad? What is the difference between a discussion group and a lynch mob? I dare say, it might just be how long you aggravate them.

In the 1950's, you could be black in the South if you were quiet or just passing through. Conversation was available with any white man. But produce a contrary view to the segregated status quo and continue to propagate that in the midst of the "gosh-darns," and you might just find yourself headed to the edge of town to check the sturdiness of a tree branch.

Calling one to another is always an attempt to create a godly reason for why we just don't live too well. It just doesn't take too much to fall into disfavor with the "gosh-darns." Sometimes just saying, "I don't agree" will get the job done. Sometimes this kind of honesty will empty a room quicker than an IRS audit.

What is within us that causes us to organize ourselves into the club of the disenfranchised? It seems to me that even the message of the Judeo-Christian philosophy boils down to, "Jesus died for us because we were such confused, miserable sinners and God was so displeased with our condition, and we were so helpless to change that He had to become a bloody mess to counteract the bloody mess we had made of things." I don't know why we find it so fun to be miserable together. What an exciting message! Where do I sign up?

So these children in the marketplace, who are sitting because they have given up on the concept of excellence and they are bored, huddle together in organizations of mutual disagreement. Well, you can't have a club without having a message to club people over the head with. So what do we need next? Well, we need a byline — a philosophy, a doctrine, a common prayer book, a pledge of allegiance, a statement of purpose. We need to prove to ourselves that the gross accumulation of our experience has legitimized our pessimistic decision.

Sitting Six
We Have Piped
and No One's Dancing

I hate to pitch a new idea to a publisher. No initial inspiration about a book can be capsulated very well. Also, you don't ever really pitch an idea to the actual publisher. There is always a front person, an editor of sorts, usually a frustrated writer, who is hired to filter out bad ideas and punch up the story lines on good ones. Case in point: arriving at the office of a publisher at about 9:00 in the morning, I led with friendliness. I know it is risky to do, because there are lots of people who enjoy splashing cold water on the warmth of others.

Such a person was Luella. She was in her mid-somethings — often hard to tell in a woman who thinks that acting old reeks of maturity. She was stern. I don't like stern. Stern, to me, is just really a mask for arrogance.

"Can I help you?"

I almost answered "no" and ran out of the building in terror, but remained, deciding not to be antisocial.

"Yes, I have an appointment to pitch an idea. I think it's a good one." I should never have added that last phrase, because I set Luella up.

"Well, we'll see about that." A curt smile.

For the next hour I pitched every story I could think of. I mean, I really think there were some good, exciting projects there. She sat, stone-faced, impassive, occasionally giving a nod — not so much a movement of the head that you could be sure. After a particularly long moment of silence, she delivered her death-knell of comment. "We tried that. It didn't sell." "It's already been done by such-and-such." And the true curse to every writer — "That sounds happy — it might make a good children's book."

Having finished my tour of duty as pitchman, I left, discouraged. She seemed to warm as I cooled. She seemed comforted by the fact that I was dejected and had lost some of my friendliness. She was content that she had done her job well. She had once again doused the hopes of an optimistic writer and established the supremacy of cynicism.

Once people collect into organizations or institutions of mutual complaint, they must discourage attempts to enlighten and refresh corporate thinking. After all, how valuable would it be to interrupt a fussiness-in-progress with some concept of how to improve the situation?

This is not limited to the secular world. We hear it in churches every Sunday. I challenge ministers who may be reading this book to pull out your last three sermons and delete every statement that includes or alludes to the following:

1. It is true that the world is filled with problems . . .
2. Because of this situation, we must be prepared to . . .
3. Although our lives are filled with many tribulations . . .
4. You may have tried everything and still not be satisfied . . .
5. I know it is difficult at times . . .
6. God knows, we try . . .
7. This is the price we pay . . .

It is time for us to understand that pity is not love and feeling sorry for yourself doesn't scare any personal demons away. There are times that even our prayers become negative reports, disclaimers. "God, we know that you are the king of the universe, that all the ways of man are filled with sorrow and distress, and that even as we pray, there are many things that you are dealing with in our world, and we cannot expect you to interrupt your busy schedule to consider our meager thoughts and words . . ."

Wow. If you think He's that busy, why waste your time in such a spiritual tizzy? Why pray? It's like putting in an application for a job at a company that's not hiring.

Now let's catch up. Jesus has said that the men of his generation are like children who emotionally haven't grown much beyond the age of thirteen, in the marketplace, thrust into an adult world filled with competition that they are ill prepared to handle. So they are sitting. Unable to compete, they have become bored with the whole tedious race. They are calling one to another — they have clumped together with people who agree with their negative assessment of planet possibilities. But now they need a doctrine. They need a common theme for their off-key nature.

What can pessimists all agree upon? "We have piped, but no one's dancing." In other words we have created elaborate pageantry and we have come up with ideas to stimulate passion within the ranks of humanity and no one cares. Our organizations have become services of repetition with occasional special projects to try to lure interest or stimulate growth. And because the members of our organizations are not motivated in any particular direction, and become poor advertisers of these special events, and because often they are too corny, contrived and redundant, repeating the same bland programming which has failed for decades — there is little response, and no one gets up to dance to our piping.

I even see this in the realm of church music. We pipe. (How appropriate, since we normally use an organ.) We sing the hymns of dead men who lived in a much more verbal, articulate time, and therefore their wording to our generation of monosyllabic men seems flowery and verbose, and who musically have pitched the tunes at such a high level that screeches are more common than tone; we sit and struggle to maintain comprehension and consciousness while in the process of singing — singing meant to produce *joy!*

Praise and worship in our churches is not a celebration of the faith experience. Rather, it is a redundant stirring of the recipe of a former time. Even when guitars and drums and horns are added, the lyrics resound with the doldrums of a people defeated, groping for the mercy of an indifferent God.

And while we're on the subject, can there be anyone more jaded than a church musician, who often plays music to no applause, having to insist that God gave the gift and "may He receive all the glory." It is a silly state of false humility. We all need appreciation. By nature we are people who creatively produce to enhance our own lives. Certainly it is a blessed perk if, in the process of enhancing our own existence and receiving appreciation for it, we can transfer some of that energy over to blessing others! But I am to love my neighbor as myself! If I feel no adulation for my efforts, no payoff for my aspirations, I certainly will not want you to be successful and happy in my midst. Get a grip! Happy people make others happy. Appreciated, talented people encourage the talent in others.

On the other hand, if we have settled for a life of mediocrity, we must quell any swell of enthusiasm towards improvement. We must become the "no way, Jose" to every foreign attempt at being positive. We will let people know that we've tried to be happy and it didn't work; even though our efforts were halfhearted or even harlequin, we still insist that we gave it the "good old college try."

True joy cannot come from compromise. Happiness does not sprout from a modicum of involvement. True praise is not conjured from a beat, nor is true worship invited by strumming a mellow melody.

Jesus said that it is possible to praise with the lips, yet the heart can remain far removed and that worship must occur because of the union of spirit *(that which has proven itself to be lasting)* and truth *(that which I have personally discovered is enriching)*.

This may all sound good, but what is our payoff for becoming motivated? Why would we want to become possessed by the notion of hope when childishness has caused us to become disappointed, and we have surrounded ourselves with people who agree with our dim outlook? For how can we welcome fresh ideas and new blood into our circle without exploding the boundaries of our thinking and causing us to come face-to-face with the reality of repentance?

Facts are, we can't. So it is safer to maintain a distance from the true music of life and instead pipe out old ideas with predictable melody lines and traditional rhyme and rhythm. The end result: no one is dancing.

Why would anyone want to dance the jitterbug for the four hundredth time? Why would anyone want to sing the songs memorized, cataloged and canonized in our minds as relics of the past? You can have the words to music in a hymnbook, a songbook, or project them on a screen — but until the children in the marketplace reject the doctrine of boredom, no one will dance. And life is about the dance.

"We have piped, but no one's dancing" because we are piping in front of the people who are calling one to another and are just like us and therefore, reflexively, give a conditioned response.

Over the years I've spoken in many churches, and I've learned that true success in ministry to any human being is to inspire that individual to escape from the tomb of his predictable reaction and expose a new emotion — one which is uncommon to him and surprises his own soul. So in some churches, just getting the congregation to laugh can be a supernal occurrence. In other churches, silencing the beat of the music and getting the gathered to be introspective can be the work of the angels. When spirituality takes hold, repetition is cast to the side. Prejudice must melt under the heat of spiritual awakening. Fresh ideas, fresh approach, fresh reaction, fresh praise — fresh people.

"We have piped but no one's dancing" is the caustic mantra of people who do not really want to change, but want you to know that they sure as tootin' did try. So what should we look for as a barometer of freshness replacing our stale activity?

1. Are we allowing new ideas and new people to confront our malaise?
2. When confronted, do we become defensive or inquisitive?
3. When hearing and viewing, do we allow ourselves to enjoy the moment?
4. While enjoying the moment, do we permit the sting of repentance to pierce our hearts?
5. While repenting, do we feel stimulated with new spirit?
6. While stimulated with new spirit, do we feel a new idea come into our own mind?

We all must be cognizant that in the pursuit of finding friendship and interaction with our fellow man we are not concluding with them that life is a futile exercise of vanity. If we would stop all of our phony piping and prefabricated programming and just sing the melody of our own life and the tune of our own dreams, people would dance. Yes, people **would** dance. And the dance would be the confirmation of the presence of God.

Sitting Seven
We Have Wept
And No One's Mourning

Jesus said, "Blessed are they that mourn, for they shall be comforted." So there is a happiness to be obtained in the process of mourning. But frequently in our language we blend words together, giving them the same definition to simplify our vocabulary. So "cry," "weep" and "mourn" have become synonymous. But are they?

Truthfully, most people cry for themselves — their losses, bruised egos and disappointment. The most common tears we ever shed are to confirm our own personal sadness. Weeping, on the other hand, is normally stimulated from an outside source — maybe concern for others and the losses that they have experienced.

But what happens if our lives have become so self-involved, so bruised by the daily struggle, that we just can't muster a tear for others? We know we need to feel for dying souls and hurting. folk in faraway lands, but it doesn't naturally occur to us to well up with tears over the anguish of another because, after all, we are children in the marketplace, sitting because we have become bored with our own endeavors, calling one to another and surrounding ourselves with people who agree with our own justifications, trying to stimulate some excitement in our lives with piping, but still seeing no dancing. Why should we care for others and weep for their difficulties when we have just decided that misery is pretty much the way life works?

Nevertheless, propriety tells us that we must attempt to manufacture some sentiment. For after all, shouldn't we mourn? What is mourning? It is a grieving due to a deep sense of loss — a heart-wrenching plea for righteous-ness and beauty to return to our lives and our times. But how can we ever achieve this level of passion or hope when we, ourselves, are not experiencing an escalation of success — when our lives have become a treadmill rather than an exhilarating jaunt? We vacillate between apathy and guilt.

So we engage the services of professionals to try to stimulate the concern, which does not naturally spring within our being. Movies. Television.

Books. They are filled with attempts to motivate great pathos to stimulate crocodile tears, trying to reach into the hardened soul and squeeze out a single drop of compassion. Sermons are preached, illuminating the agony of the crucifixion and the deaths of martyrs to facilitate a moment's reflection of something other than the vision of our own plight. Evangelists, politicians, and motivational speakers — all attempt to dent the armor of protection we have donned to alleviate the deep wounds and sorrow from touching our flesh. Somewhere in our sanctum of soul there is still the nagging voice saying, "Ask not for whom the bell tolls — it tolls for thee."

Yet it is difficult to hear the bells when our own self-interest chimes so loudly in our heads. In our more enlightened moments we know that each man's pain diminishes us and should reach deep into our hearts. But we can't. We are too concerned over our own inadequacies and tender spots. So the cynicism sinks deeper. That which is an attempt to remind us of our weakness often just leaves us cold and frustrated with our dilemma and perturbed with those who have tried to crack our nut.

Churches attempt to actuate repentance by simulating death experiences and talking of the horrors of hell and telling anecdotes of the misery produced by iniquity. But no one's mourning. And Jesus says because they cannot legitimately mourn, they cannot be comforted. For mourning by its very nature is a belief that God sees our tears and he cares and is moving to change the injustice. But what if you don't believe that God really cares for you as a person in the here and now? What if you think religion is a ticket for the afterlife, a passage for eternity, not a philosophy for living today? Then what is the use for tears? If tears are only going to bring deeper reflection, why weep? How much bewilderment is there in the heart of God over a people who are tear-free because they do not really believe there is any comfort? This is perhaps the pinnacle of cynicism. The "gosh-darns" contend, "Why give a damn when giving a damn doesn't really do a damn thing?"

Thus the introduction of the practice of "surfing" — skimming the surface of everything in our lives — just as we surf the Internet. We surface praise, worship, sorrow — only allowing tears to creep into the corners of our eyes when we ourselves have been offended. But the Bible does not say that self-seeking tears are comforted; it does not say that weeping is comforted. Only when it becomes spontaneous mourning — a deep, soul stirring, out-pouring of tears, does it reach the heart of God and cause him to introduce the Comforter, His Holy Spirit.

So, in actuality, what really destroys the integrity of a human being? Neutralizing both joy *and* sadness, leaving the person overly calm and unmoved. The fault does not lie with the Bible or with the teachings of Jesus. Actually, his words are waiting to be interpreted by daring souls who wish to feel instead of just react. The problem lies in our dubious attempts to simulate spirituality by inserting religiosity, which is promptly rejected by the thirsty soul who deep in the inward parts knows the difference between water and kerosene.

But once we've reached the point where we have rejected the validity of mourning and therefore have not received our gift of spiritual tenderness, we are incapable of recognizing the true message of God brought by his prophets.

Sitting Eight
J the B

At this point Jesus introduces a new character, a controversial figure of his time dubbed John the Baptist. I am really curious about this maneuver. So far in the parable he had been speaking in generalities, his most specific reference being about men. Why introduce a living character? Perhaps it is because, in the midst of any commentary, dismal as it may seem, God is always hatching a new scheme. While people are becoming mediocre and too commonplace for their own good, there is always someone that God calls from the pack to become the prophet of their age. Such a man was John the Baptist.

John possessed all the elements necessary for a prophetic message. Let me be clear about this — prophetic messages don't restate present spiritual truths or present a clever nuance in thinking. Prophets by their very nature dissect all sections of humankind, never focusing on the spiritual more than the practical, nor the eternal more than the earthly. They come to remind us of our created self — the part of us which is the image of God. They taunt and tease us into seeing the fallacy in our normal living. They develop a style contrary to popular etiquette; God knows, maybe even obtuse to conventional morality. They are not here to reform; they have been given an edict to "lay the axe to the root." They are not interested in approval; matter of fact, often in their own times, they are voices crying in the wilderness (if you didn't know, the wilderness is not the most excellent venue for gathering a crowd). Prophets always bring something new in approach and revolutionary in substance.

For John it was baptism. Jesus followed suit, baptizing his own converts. Baptism — what is it? We have e-therealized the action to symbolize union with God or cleansing from sin, but initially it was just something bizarre and controversial to do to prove that converts had separated themselves from traditional Jewish thinking. It was not the custom of the Jews to baptize anyone, so John made it the vanguard of his movement.

Baptism, rather than merely being the symbolism of accepting God, is actually a radical emersion into a new philosophy — a total departure from conventional thinking. Prophets have three characteristics in common. Their message is always:

1. We can do better.
2. What we are doing right now has lost all of its meaning.
3. If we don't change what we're doing, we will perish in our own stupidity.

It is the role of intelligent, spiritual beings to recognize these prophets, acknowledge their message, and incorporate bits and pieces of the more powerful thoughts into the common man's lingo.

Jesus himself did this. Not only did he borrow baptism itself from John, he began his ministry just down the river on the Jordan and also adopted John's message for his byline: "Repent for the Kingdom of God is at hand." Jesus was even baptized by John to establish the validity of the emerging spirit. Jesus stated that there was no one born of woman who was greater than John, but cleverly inserted that he who is least in the Kingdom is greater than John.

So the reason Jesus brings up John the Baptist at this point is that, predictably, John was a source of great conflict and debate amongst the people who were listening to Jesus' parable. John had no mercy on the religious system. Even when the religious leaders came out to partake of his baptism, he chased them away and told them they should go home and produce some evidence in their lives that they were even worthy to be a part of the new Godly escapade — obviously, not the best way to win friends and influence people. But it is the only way to produce the elements of reasoning which "egg on" debate and accelerate spiritual revival.

So I suppose I don't need to tell you that children in the marketplace who were sitting and calling one to another, complaining about how they had piped and mourned and no one was listening, were not particularly drawn to the message of a prophet who liked to dip his grasshoppers in honey before he devoured them. But that is the way of life. Someone has to make the "gosh darns" nervous to prepare the soil for new growth.

I believe this is made clear in the teachings of Jesus when he tells his disciples that unless they hate their mother and father they will not enter the Kingdom of God. I stop and smile when I think of the number of preachers who have tried to explain that one away. But please understand, placed deep in the soul of every child is an instinct for freedom from existing mores, and a natural revulsion to repetitive behavior. The result is a cleansing within every generation of outdated policy and a genetic purging of the vice and silliness which leads us to become just like those who have flopped before us.

Without children naturally rebelling against their parents, and prophets reminding us of our better selves, we will soon settle in to mundanity and fiercely defend it to the destruction of all that is holy and good.

John the Baptist *was* a prophet, but we have them today, too. Jesus made it clear that he, (Jesus) had "children" that we don't even know about. They are in the entertainment industry, politics, government, schools, music — every walk of life.

So what is a prophet? Anybody who gains a voice and is not worried about an audience but instead declares the futility of childishness and the pursuit of excellence, brings great profit to the human spirit and shall receive a prophet's reward.

These are not people to be worshipped and extolled but rather to be admired and imitated. So you think you might want to be a prophet? Then don't wait for your own message. Pick up the words of the local seer and doer in your own community. Find those who fearlessly speak against procedures that give us only status with no quo. Borrow their message and emulate their actions that create change. In so doing, you not only grant yourself the tremendous blessing of being involved, but you give credibility to a noble adventure. Because if you don't, the "gosh-darns" around you will pressure you to find fault and attack the inspired messenger.

Sitting Nine
It's of the Devil

John did have one major flaw. He tried to be different while at the same time desperately attempt to please the people by doing without food and drink — fasting — acting like a good Jewish boy. But prophets can't jump into the soup of a community; God is always stirring a new broth. So even though John was very Jewish, because he did not condone the mediocrity of his day, the people came to a conclusion. "He has a devil."

This was the beginning of an ongoing game amongst the "gosh-darns." When in doubt, blame the devil. It has become an unholy tradition. It really is quite simple. If we are not doing it, our brothers are not doing it, our families are not doing it, and our church has never seen it, it must be of the devil. If we can insist that every new movement has been forged in the fiery pit of hell we can proclaim it against God's ways. Therefore we don't have to deal with it. Perhaps you have noticed that religious broadcasting contains more advertising on the workings of the dark side than it ever does with words to enlighten the troops of righteousness.

One night I had one lady ask me if I believed in the devil.

"Why? Is he starting a church?" I queried.

"No, I just want to find out if you're a Bible-believing Christian."

"So if I believe in the devil, I'm a good Christian?"

"No, it just means you believe the whole word of God."

"Let me tell you, ma'am, I don't give the devil a helluva lot of thought."

She walked away, disgusted with me in more ways than I want to think about. She was a believer in the great scapegoat of all man's stupidity: "It's the devil." I can hear it now!
"I didn't get the job. The devil must be in charge of personnel." (Of course, there's the possibility that you just didn't do good work.) "My car broke down. The devil's after me." (Or you forgot to change your oil every 3500 miles.)

Whatever you believe about evil, darkness or Satan, in the long run, it doesn't amount to a hill of beans. This is why Jesus said, "Get thee behind me, Satan." I don't know — that might be

76

translated today as "kiss my ass." And before you get offended by that, understand that Jesus' mission was to destroy all the works of the devil, and certainly primary amongst his works is his overly exaggerated sense of importance.

"John the Baptist came neither eating or drinking, and you say he has a devil." Can't you just see the twinkle in Jesus' eye when he said that? You see, for the "gosh-darns" devil talk is an awesome, quick solution. For if John is of the devil, then all those nasty sermons he delivered about us can be dismissed as satanic. Therefore, I'm okay, you're okay — he's possessed. It sounds like a great title for a new book to help us recover from the trauma of anyone who questions the validity of sameness.

So is there a devil? I sure see some awfully hellish things — like the old biddy, scrunching her face up like a prune when the black man and white woman walk by carrying their beautiful baby. It's devilish when children are told to stop asking so many questions about God because we're really not meant to know the answers. Hell sure seems real when people refuse to give money to homeless people because they're sure they'll use it to buy liquor, or when ministers preach the party line when they know it has no substance or value to their congregations. Yes, I see the horns and pointy tails on every bigoted man who expresses his supremacy over another man based upon race, creed, color or sexual preference. I sniff the brimstone of hell every time a political leader tells me we must go off and kill some foreign infidel to keep the sanctity of our freedom. It seems that Satan doesn't scare me as much as fools in power. It's just too easy for people who are childish and bored, who are clinging to each other, hoping to maintain their sanctuary of servitude to become vindictive against those who would just like to guzzle some cooler refreshment from the fountain of life. "It's of the devil" has caused more heartache and less true revival than any phrase ever uttered.

So if we become too intensely involved in maintaining the integrity of our own wishy-washy existence, what else can we do but reject any soul with the audacity to suggest otherwise? John had a message from God but tried to honor the traditions of his people. It did him no good. They still rejected his message as coming from the fires of hell. Even John recommended that we find contentment. But there is a true danger in allowing ourselves to become complacent. Contentment is working with what we've been given. Complacency, on the other hand, is settling for our own work.

Remember: John was a forerunner, an opening act for a much more intense message to follow. Here comes . . .

Sitting Ten
The Son of Man

Jesus Christ. Type the two words on a piece of paper, and no one knows if you mean something profane or profound; perhaps not that different from the man himself. After 2,000 years of accumulated disinformation, separating the man from the myth and the message from the theology is a task best suited for angels, not scholars, theologians, or especially bawdy, fault-ridden writers like myself. Still, aptly fitting the qualification of one of those who rushes in where angels fear to trod, I would like to address the issue of Jesus Christ, who actually preferred to be called the Son of Man.

The main difficulty in talking about Jesus is that he has become the poster child for every denominational subtlety, religious atrocity, rock and roll video or cathedral fresco for so many years that his name conjures too many images and too many mixed emotions to draw a correct bead on the heart and the soul of the man. Perhaps it would be best to look at the things he believed about himself.

80

First and foremost, the young Nazarene wanted to be recognized and appreciated for his words. Perhaps his words would have been better re-membered if the stories of his miracles had not been so outstandingly published. I guess it's similar to the plumber who really wants to be a poet, but as long as he is so doggone good at cleaning drains, no one wants to read his verse. But at the heart of the man, Jesus was a resolute revolutionary who believed there was a message required that was earth-ready and people-friendly. Today we skim across his words, mostly relegating them to the status of Hallmark card niceties, never understanding that the manifesto he presented was not about heavenly achievement, but mostly and more importantly, about earthly interaction. So forgive my digression. Back to what he believed for and about himself:

1. Primal was "do unto others as you would have them do unto you." We have tritely referred to this as the Golden Rule. Honestly, it is the *only* rule. What sets Jesus apart from other great religious leaders is that he really did not desire to establish a kingdom, confiscate a people, free a culture or provide divine guidance for eternal destinations. Heaven is a conclusion best left to the Creator, our Father. But the Son of Man had a mission to give us a message that would recreate heaven in our dealings here on earth.

"Do unto others as you would have them do unto you" is not an option. If I live my life only for myself, I am outnumbered six billion to one. I become the only person who really cares what I feel and is pursuing what I need. I have 6 billion neighbors who don't really give a crap about me. But if there are 6 billion people on this planet who are discovering what they really want in their lives and projecting that same interest to the fellows around them, we all have the potential for 6 billion people to be just as concerned about our situation as we are.

"An eye for an eye and a tooth for a tooth" is not a philosophy. It is a retribution — making everyone who disagrees with us our mortal enemy. The problem in the Middle East is not insurmountable. Battle lines are drawn and targets are established — so much so that it has become ingrained in the genetic code of all the locals.

To say that every religion in the world teaches the same thing that Jesus teaches is ludicrous. Jesus said, "Out of the abundance of the heart (emotions) the mouth speaks." Yet a Buddhist will tell you that only by neutralizing the passions does truth emerge. Can I actually neutralize my passions? And if I can, why would I want to? Why are we so ashamed about being emotionally — based people? Jesus said we exist as beings with heart, soul, mind and strength, but that the doorway to every human is the heart — the emotions. It is what we all lead with, unless we are trying to disguise our humanity behind some philosophical blunder-buss. From the heart we allow our souls to be reached and then the soul can renew the mind, energizing the body with ideas.

2. *"I have not come to condemn the world, but to seek and save that which is lost."* Lost. What an absolutely fabulous word. Doesn't that describe our futile flailing at the air, attempting to explain our inconsistency? And Jesus doesn't just want to merely save us, he wants to seek us, woo us, understand us, court us, and discover us as we unveil ourselves. Any attempt to transform this message into a dogmatic, moralistic code of religious or social behavior is not only out of step with the reality of Jesus' life and mission, but abominable.

3. "I have come to bring life and full joy." There it is again — excitement and happiness. Why are we so intent on living a life without them? Why have we allowed ourselves to be deceived into believing we must steal moments of pleasure instead of lavishing ourselves in glorious joy? Why have we lost our sense of humor about ourselves, thinking we appear adult by developing excuse upon excuse for our ongoing mishaps?

I think it is safe to say that someone who believes in abundant life and full joy is not going to be picky about an occasional mistake. I think Jesus believed that the quality of life is much more important than the quantity of rightness.

4.   "Be of good cheer." He said it all the time. He really wanted us to keep a sense of sanity by laughing at the attempts by life to make everything deathly serious. Whether drowning in a boat, dying of a disease, being possessed by a demon, or just greeting a friend, he strongly suggested keeping perspective by having great cheer in our lives. You would have to agree: this is not the lifestyle of a stoic philosopher. This is the message of a man seething with practical optimism and blossoming with each declaration of hope.

5. **"*Don't call me good.*"** A young ruler approached Jesus one day and called him "good master." He deflected the salutation and praise by saying, "Why do you call me good? There is none good but God." It is in the very DNA of our species to despise haughtiness and pride but the "gosh-darns" *encourage* it under the guise of self-worth and self-appreciation. Jesus' philosophy was to do great things and then blow them off. When he'd heal a man, he would request that he tell no one. He entered into Jerusalem riding on a donkey to the adulation of the masses. If that is not a sardonic moment, please tell me what the meaning was. Goodness is never achieved by proclamation, blooming instead, through observation and time.

6. **"*Your faith has made you whole.*"** Although blessed with powers and anointing, he refused to take credit for the healings in men's lives. Instead he showed them — and us — that the choices we make and the belief we express at the right moments determine our outcome and enhance our opportunities. Did their faith really make them whole, or was this just promo jive from a well-versed con man? All we do know is that when he went to his home town, Nazareth, and the people did not believe in him, Jesus was not able to help them. So he didn't lie — the fact of the matter is, he taught us that God requires us to bring five loaves and two fishes before five thousand are ever fed. He taught us that faith must be in place before action will occur.

7. *"Greater things shall you do because I go to the Father."* Certainly doesn't sound like the words of a puny, insecure preacher-man. But there are things that did make him paranoid. What made Jesus suspicious? What made his skin crawl? What made him hostile and angry? Religious hypocrites who forced their will and superiority on the common man to gain spiritual and financial advantage. Jesus was a great brother because he hoped we would do better than he did. I can't love someone who only wants me to be his fan and doesn't hope and pray that I excel.

We certainly have discussed the profound nature of Jesus' message, but within that character was an individual who was tired of form with no reason and piety with no purpose.

For instance, what an easy thing it would have been for him to wash his hands before he ate like all the Jews did! But he refused. How difficult would it have been for him to cease teaching and healing on the Sabbath to please existing religious practice? He refused. How intelligent would it have been of him, in a promotional sense, to receive one of the leaders of the religious community, Nicodemus, with open arms and universal acceptance? He refused. Instead he told the vacillating Pharisee who came to him under the cover of night that he must be born again.

To continue: how simple would it have been to present his teachings as insights instead of edicts from the heavenly Father? The Jews would have welcomed including Jesus into their rituals and worship! He refused. Why not pass over dinner invitations with known criminals, felons and outcasts? He refused and instead, flaunted it before their noses. How difficult would it have been to honor the traditions of the day by pigeonholing women in servant positions instead of including them into the inner circle of teaching and ministering as equals? He refused. How popular could he have been if he had called whores and prostitutes abominations to God, instead of saying that they would enter the Kingdom before the religious leaders? He refused. How easy would it have been to escape the bumbling arresting officers in the garden of Gethsemane and return to Galilee to minister to friendlier sorts? He refused.

To the average orthodox Jews of his day, Jesus was a profane and foul-tempered sinner, ransacking their temple and luring their fine young sons and daughters out into the wilderness for communal living. But you see, he was the Son of Man. They wanted a king of the Jews. They besought a Jewish Messiah. But he came to be an elder brother to all the sons and daughters of planet Earth.

Sitting Eleven
Eating and Drinking

I can usually tell by looking at the glassy stare that comes over the eyes — it is the appearance people have right before they blink and nod off. This was the look on my son's face when I was trying to explain geometry to him. All of us reach a point of mental saturation — we just can't take any more. But we're afraid to admit what we're hearing is not being mentally digested. So often you have children who have been unleashed into the marketplace, unprepared for the path set before them. They are sitting, bored stiff with the struggle of life. In response, they huddle into little groups for reassurance, complaining about how they have tried everything and nothing really works. They make fun or grumble about those who promote difference.

So what is their fate? What is left of these people who have given up on the passions of their own dreams and seem totally bewildered by the true purpose of the human soul?

What is left is the body. We
worship the body. We fuss over the body.
People who will talk of nothing else will
discuss their physicalities with you with
great fluidity. Just bring up the subject of
food, and watch people launch into
discussions of fat grams, carbohydrates,
nutritional values, vitamins, minerals and
antioxidants. Is it not ironic that in a
generation that lacks excitement and
happiness, often the main thrill is to
extend that existence through better
health, medication and nutrition? We
actually believe that what we eat and what
we drink makes more difference than how
we digest it.

Jesus said, "It's not what comes into
the body that defiles a man, but what
comes out of the body." Now, I know he
was referring to actions of the heart, but if
you think about it, the digestive system is
the most powerful organ and process in
the human being — much more delicate
than the heart, glands, lungs and limbs. It
affects every portion of our makeup and is
affected by every temperament of our
thinking.

Is it possible that we can eat
nutritious food and be so discontented
that we digest it poorly, thereby creating
the climate for all sorts of disorders?

Don't get me wrong — I believe in good eating habits. I get my five fruits and vegetables every day, but I know very well that nothing settles well in my stomach, even broccoli and oatmeal, when my soul is distressed and my heart is confounded.

Perhaps much disease could be eliminated by easing the emotional heart instead of medicating the physical one. There is nothing wrong with medicine, and there is nothing wrong with being treated for disorders, and certainly nothing wrong with a good diet, but they are not replacements for finding a permanent peace that stills the churning innards and allows the good things we eat to enrich us.

People in Jesus' day were mad at him because he ate and drank. They were mad because his disciples didn't fast and do all those religious things that people do to communicate that they are adequately miserable in their walk with God. Jesus' reply was, "Why should they fast? I am here, they're here, we're happy — what's the problem?"

When the freedom that other people enjoy in life causes you to be suspicious and festers a knot in your stomach, it will not be the fat grams that kill you. If we are truly and internally a physical representation of what we emotionally and spiritually have launched within, then many souls are already contorting with disease. We must learn to digest information and food with the same grace in our whole being — heart, soul, mind and strength.

Eating and drinking were never meant to be a lifestyle. They were planned as blessings, nutrients, and even celebration. But to make our food welcome, we must make our souls receptive.

Sitting Twelve
Wine-Bibbers, Gluttons
And a Friend of Sinners

"Misery loves company." What a chilling statement! Is it true? Do we really think that people will be benefited by acquiring our choices? Do we really feel like evangelizing people so they may achieve our emotional status? Or is it all just an inglorious façade, that since we have to love God and go the church, everyone should have to love God and go to church? It was the same thing in Jesus' day — the people, many of them not particularly religious — still wanted Jesus and his disciples to follow a code of ethics and behavior. When they saw him eating, drinking wine, and partying with known sinners, they objected vehemently. When he refused to toe the line, they were indignant — not so different from today. It has become a bizarre tradition in our country to discredit people who would dare to have more fun than we have. We are suspicious of happiness and excitement, and prefer a controlled, morose, sober-mindedness.

We even medicate ourselves to achieve this. Pills are given to "knock off the edges" of personality, to make people fit in better with the melancholy masses.

But Jesus was not ashamed to enjoy life and party. This made him suspect and caused the people to be critical of him. More accurately, it made them jealous of his freedom.

I guess it all comes down to this issue: ***whose business is sin?*** Until we resolve this question in our minds, we are dangerous to everyone who crosses our path — never truly clear whether we are friend or foe. We leave people in limbo based upon our approval or disapproval of their quirks. But whose business is sin? Jesus said we are not to judge. I believe that includes all the cantankerous synonyms for the word — evaluate, assess, critique, review, appraise, estimate, rate, rank, censure, rule, discern, discriminate, or even consider. Many people will disagree with me, thinking that the synonyms are important in the process of separating the sheep from the goats and the wheat from the tares, but Jesus basically said that the separating process would be done after death, at the judgment day, not in some church boardroom or parlor filled with bewitched women.

Being judgmental does not create happy people. There is a wonderful freedom that comes into the human experience when we no longer care to hear all the gossip and the tales of someone else's questionable doings. May I be the first to say, I just don't care who is zooming who. I learned a long time ago, there is nothing easier in the world than sex. For God's sake, *monkeys* do it. It is a strong urge, and I no longer want to hear who is denying the urge and who is answering it. I wish to remain happy and excited. My request? Leave me in my euphoria of non-complaining. I do not believe this is idealism; I believe idealism exists in the minds of those puny, straight-laced and narrow-minded individuals who think they can control the morality of themselves, let alone others. I do not even think that "don't ask, don't tell" brings peace of mind. I recommend, "Get a life and don't think about it." Jesus was content and overjoyed with his passage. He made a great guest for a party. He made a great guest to go fishing with. He is a terrific comrade to have on a long trip. And you never have to worry about talking with him and wondering if he's going to "spill the beans."

Whose business is sin? I don't know if even God cares, because the Bible says that grace covers a multitude of sins. You may feel free to preach against sin all you want, but no one will ever give up what they have until they are guaranteed something better. We are just not very good at not sinning. Certainly we should learn from our mistakes and grow, but "willpower" is something that Will has, but no one else. My Jonathan power does not keep me from error, but by the grace of God, it does keep me from judgment because I religiously stay away from judgmental people. Lest you try to become clever and insist that I am judging the judgmental, it's just that my head spins when I listen to people discuss right and wrong.

Case in point: recently a fellow at a church said that one of my friends looked like a homosexual. What is that look? And what type of mind knows what to look for? What kind of twisted, self-righteous, foul-spirited being knows what look will stimulate homosexuality? And how can we make judgments on such issues? Especially when we live in stained glass houses? For if you closed all the churches in America, incest would decrease by at least 70%. Every time I go to a jailhouse to minister, some 95% of the prisoners have come from strong religious backgrounds. It seems to me we have a public relations problem. If our churches cannot produce a better batch of people, where do we ever get off thinking we can judge the actions of the world? Jesus said he *could* judge, and his judgment would be righteous and fair, but he refused to do it, leaving that job to God and God alone.

I am weary of self-righteousness. I am weary of rules that do not produce gleaming examples of soul satisfaction. I am queasy over teaching that instructs in procedures of practice without ever laying the groundwork for motivation.

This brings us back to Jesus. How do you get to be a friend of sinners? For you see, that's what the "gosh-darns" of his day accused Jesus of being. The "gosh-darns" — those childish, bored, cliquish, judgmental folk who hide behind their own fears and inadequacies by shouting disapproval at people trying to make a difference — they were angry at Jesus because he was a friend of sinners. Back to our question: how do you get to be a friend of sinners? Honestly, you don't get to be a friend of sinners by telling them they're going to hell — not a crowd pleaser. A friend of sinners is someone who lives an excited and happy life in the midst of unhappy and bored people who are not "gosh-darns" and are still searching for more.

Did Jesus drink grape juice or wine? What difference does it make? If you are looking for purity and religious reverence in the life of Jesus, you are, at the very least, going to find an enigma, because, although he loved God, he loved life, and asked God in the Garden of Gethsemane, to grant him more of it.

What prompts us to be so interested in the gory details? Why do we need to know the dirty facts of every mistake made by our fellow man? Maybe it's because we are so constricted and repressed that we are incapable of really juicy sins for ourselves and must read about them in vivid accounts so that we can pretend to cringe at the shamelessness of it all as we buy another copy of the tabloid to learn even more slimy stuff.

Is there anyone that can really cast the first stone? The notion that Jesus was sinless was one of those contentions that occurred long after his death. Certainly none of the disciples thought he was sinless when he was cursing fig trees and yelling at them about their lack of faith. The religious leaders of the day made it clear to everyone that they believed he was a sinner. Truthfully, that accusation was better for advertising his message than any sermon he ever preached, because once lost people know that we are not in the back pocket of religious practitioners, and that our arms are open wide in acceptance, they will run to find answers and safe haven within our embrace.

Take a moment, suck up some air, and admit to yourself, there are just times when you need to be left alone and not be evaluated by every Reverend Tom, Pastor Dick and Rabbi Harry. After all, it was Jesus who gave us the image of God as a good earthly father. It was Jesus who gave us the presentation of God as a great host at a banquet. It was Jesus who came to show us the father, and if we are to understand what the father is really like, it is to be found in the character and the compassion of his son, Jesus.

Jesus — who was not afraid of sinners. Jesus — who became angry at the worship of relics over the relishing of humankind. Jesus — who took all the criticism and intimidation of his day, and told the religious that they were hypocrites because they cleaned the outside of their cups, but the inside was filthy. He told them that they painted their tombstones to make them shiny and bright, but inside were dead men's bones.

It is the nature of childish, bored, egocentric and judgmental people to deprive everyone of pleasure as a punishment for their own lives being so devoid of enjoyment. It is Jesus who still stands at the door of the church and knocks, hoping that we will allow some liberty and freedom to enter. It is Jesus, the winebibber, glutton and friend of sinners, who has a message of acceptance and inclusion for all people.

Whose business is sin? Frankly, my dear, I don't give a damn . . .

Sitting Thirteen
Wisdom Is Justified of All of Her Children

In this day and age, arriving in the grocery store, one is normally presented or accosted, depending upon your particular mood, with a barrage of individuals offering samples of free food. Would you like to try this? Would you like to try that? I have to admit, sometimes I'm elated at the prospect of the neat nibbles, and at times, I would like to be left alone. But at least, I must admire the intelligence of the companies who make products that no one has ever really tasted before, so they know they must give little pieces of their parcels away to stimulate interest and create a market. Can you imagine if they just offered a new kind of chicken in the frozen food section — they could build a beautiful advertising campaign, offer special prices and print all sorts of testimonials, but the chicken would probably not cluck.

People need one of two pieces of information to become enthusiastic about a new idea. They either need a friend or loved one who becomes passionate about the product to stimulate their interest, or even offer some, or they need to personally experience it for themselves — the actual taste landing on their palate. You can advertise to them, promote or even tease them—but until you give them the experience that pleases them, they are not only unconvinced but also totally disinterested.

Jesus finishes his parable by saying that in his generation he sees that people have childishly failed to emotionally mature, leaving them destitute of the energy necessary to compete in the marketplace of life, so naturally they become intimidated and eventually escape into boredom. Being bored, they further seek confirmation of their adequacy by surrounding themselves with people who "amen" their assessment of the game. Conversation for these accumulated, despaired individuals nor-mally centers around the futility of trying to do something when nothing seems to work. This cult of the "gosh-darns," as we dubbed them, develops mutual enemies — any individual who tries to introduce excitement and happiness into the equation. They become overly critical because it temporarily gives them a sense of being God, which makes them become overly religious as long as the theory of religion is discussed and not the practical application. They become fearful because change is a shocking prospect in a life established in a tiny cubicle of limited interaction. They are touchy and sensitive because their own hearts prod them to deeper concerns, so they certainly do not want to be motivated by outside forces and voices which would ally themselves with their own prickly consciences. They become judgmental because the danger of introducing new ideas and new people, or new standards and mores causes them to reflect on their own insecurities. They are susceptible to any power of suggestion that promotes the preservation of the ongoing blandness. They seek a common thread to form the garment of mediocrity among all of their acquaintances. Their conversations may aspire to praise and, the discovery of truth, but eventually degenerate to the criticism of wayward philosophies and the hounding of souls deemed weaker and less acceptable. They shudder at the thought of change.

Growing older, they commit the worst atrocity of all. They become nostalgic. Really, the only value of

growing older is the accumulation of some
financial security and, through viewing
one's own mistakes, becoming more
tolerant of others. Nostalgia is an attempt
to stop speeding traffic on the freeway by
merely lifting one's hand — futile and
dangerous.

So, at a time in our lives when aging
should produce maturity and compassion,
the "gosh-darns" become a people with
concrete attitudes and features. Bom-
barding them with information or
exposing them to cultural experience is
paramount to serving caviar to dogs.
Some of them may eat it but lament that
the jelly is not sweet enough. Most of
them will either refuse to partake or spit it
out because of preconceived preferences.

This is why Jesus says that if we
think we have found a piece of wisdom, to
use preaching or teaching to propel that
concept is certainly the weakest form of
communication. Wisdom needs time and
freedom to spawn offspring — children.

And may I add, it needs keen
powers of timing and observation. There
was a rare opportunity for the church in
the South in the late 1960s. Integration
having been legally imposed on the
masses, there was a door of opportunity
to make it seem as if it were an idea

birthed from our religious loins instead of forced by national decree. The truth of the matter is, the Southern church did nothing to prevent segregation throughout the forties, fifties and early sixties. By then it had become obvious that this arcane system was doomed to failure. If, at that point, they had taken even two minutes to read the scriptural position on racial equality, the ministers and congregations of our Southern states could have become, if not the forerunners, at least the late-runners for a truly inspired and necessary transition.

If they had done this, and had begun to preach from the pulpit the wisdom of racial interaction and the evils of bigotry, we would have a generation today of children reared in that era who are now in charge of businesses and government who would be practically free of prejudicial thinking. *Every great idea is parented by one generation and acted out by the next.*

The fact of the matter is that the church was reticent to accept integration and only gradually became an advocate for its validity. Because of that choice, a generation of baby boomers in a Southern culture who could have been free of judgmentalism are now in a nervous state of racial ambiguity. They just don't know what to think, so they don't think about it much, and nothing really changes.

On the other hand, there were no black people in America in the 1940s who didn't know, deep in their hearts, that they were just as equal in God's eyes as any white man. Unfortunately, that knowledge did them no good. But they fostered the notion and taught it to their children in their small churches and gatherings, not allowing themselves to become victimized by the stupidity and foul thinking of the present day. They chose simple statements, as exemplified in the philosophy of Rosa Parks. "Let me just sit in the front of a bus." For you see, rational people, although they tolerated segregation, found it difficult to think that a woman should be jailed because of where she sat on a bus. Or that a group of young people should be refused service at a diner. Even though these things were common practice in the segregationist South, people who maintained reason questioned the wisdom and authority of such maneuvers. Yet, had these black leaders become violent and forced larger issues that were more controversial, their cause would have been squelched by the antipathy of the mass of the white "gosh-darns." Simple ideas, simple practice, great results. The black community taught wisdom to their children well. The children, in turn, chose their causes well. They won some victories.

Wisdom needs a place to grow where it can influence people who will impregnate the beauty of an idea in their own lives, their own dealings, and the fertile minds of their children. Without that, ideas appear and they are aborted by the pressing, critical "gosh-darns."

Jesus made it clear that precious time is wasted trying to wrangle position and wheedle deals with existing systems. We knew this in the late sixties. We knew that the existing philosophy of materialism and the political climate of imperialism was wrong. Our parents told us to work within the boundaries. We disagreed. Instead we constructed a sub-culture. Whether you agree with all the tenets of the hippie philosophy or not, you have to acknowledge that it became instrumental in dismantling the Vietnam War machine and dethroning a very perverse and crooked administration.

Then something dastardly happened. These seekers of change became civilized, bored and overwrought with their own sense of self-importance and intoxicated by sexual liberation and the pursuit of money. They justified their actions by saying they had decided to "just work within the system." And behold, they became what they beheld.

Wisdom needs time and intellectual purity to create an offspring to offset the mongrel thinking which has stagnated us in a cesspool of stoppage. When we are young, fresh and virile, we breed. The same thing is true mentally and emotionally. When you tell someone that they can achieve more than what they presently see, and you give them a climate of liberty to do that, they will father a new notion and mother that experience to maturity.

I believe a de-escalation of creativity occurs because of the message we preach. The problem in all of our religious system is that we want to establish *divinity* before we have ever established *affinity*. And it is not just the divinity of God and his Christ, but also the divinity of the Bible, the divinity of our cause, the divinity of our religious leaders and the divinity of our relics and practices. Honestly, I don't really care if Jesus is divine if he's not relevant. I don't think I'm alone in believing that force-feeding me globs of goop that I am supposed to accept by faith is not my idea of fine, spiritual dining.

Just sit down and tell me who Jesus is. Tell me why Jesus is. Better yet, tell me how Jesus is. Let me grow affectionate for the man before you crown him as a god. Religion is weakened by its need for quiet, reverent followers. Religion is rendered insipid by an unwillingness to be questioned. Religion becomes a mockery when it produces no product but demands weekly service. Religion becomes the national joke when it produces no offspring from its wisdom, rather birthing a series of bastard attempts at campaigns and crusades. Religion loses its power by prostituting itself with political causes that fade into history quicker than the hula-hoop.

Jesus refuses to argue with the "gosh-darns." Jesus refuses to reason with the "gosh-darns". Because, honestly, the only way a religious person ever raises his blood pressure is when he defends his position. If you refuse to argue with religion, it will soon be lulled back into sleep. There was no need for Jesus to bicker with the religious leaders of his day. In less than forty years, their system of religious practice and their orderly boredom was destroyed by the Roman legions and the people scattered throughout the world.

Wisdom needs an offspring. Therefore it needs a chance to court, date, marry and procreate. Sometimes this takes only a little while and sometimes it takes generations. But the purity of the concept needs to remain. Jesus makes it clear to the people that we must learn the difference between truths which are eternal and politically correct positions which are the passing fancy of a given time.

It reminds me of a story. One day when the disciples were asking Jesus about divorce, he told them that Moses granted them the right to divorce out of the hardness of their hearts. He said it really wasn't God's idea — it was Moses' idea. But that Mosaic edict about divorce is in our Bible, and we are taught that it is the inspired word of God. Well, guess what? It isn't. The philosophy of divorce has neither stood the test of time, nor has its wisdom produced an offspring of flourishing children. Although perhaps necessary at times, it is still a painful human process, not recommended for general consumption.

Wisdom needs a chance to breed in a pure environment, free of restrictive interference. I know in our time it is popular to become more conservative, but the very definition of the term means to conserve, maintain and revere a present status quo instead of seeking for new ways to address the human grievance.

Innovative thinking needs time to become necessary action and culminate in practical wisdom. Every new invention, every freedom, every equality, every spiritual inspiration, every musical innovation, every theatrical discovery, every governmental improvement, and every human enhancement—first began as a radical concept, viciously attacked by the existing "gosh-darns."

If change spends all of its time arguing with the "gosh-darns", it will exhaust itself and have no energy to input life and our times when opportunity arises. Save your strength. Save your mind. Save your energy. Wisdom will get its crack.

Isn't that what Jesus meant in the Beatitudes when he said that the meek shall inherit the earth? Honestly, you do not inherit anything until something else dies. Remember, the "gosh-darns" have one obvious weakness — they get bored easily. Their goals die quickly, and then you can quietly step in and inherit the opportunity they have abandoned. Argue with them, they become stronger. Ignore them, and they become bored.

This is the Jesus way.

He takes the high road in the sense that having explained the situation he observed in his generation, he chose to walk away from the fray and build a kingdom not of this world. Yes, I like that. The true kingdom of God is always "out of sight" but never out of mind.

Sitting Fourteen
I Knew Jesus before
He Was a Christian

Sometimes a word just gets worn out. It has been squeezed into so many diverse jobs that it ceases to have any practical definition or application. Such a word is *Christian*.

I am a firm believer in the life, times and all the philosophies and claims of Jesus. But I have just come to the conclusion that Jesus would make a lousy Christian. He was uncomfortable with ritual. He hated judgmentalism. Hypocrisy made him so mad that he became violent and whipped people. He found it impossible to be dogmatic, saying, "Those that are not against us are for us."

Let us think rationally. Christianity has committed too many atrocities and applauded too many fools to be taken seriously as either a word or a movement. Maybe when they first used the word in Antioch so many centuries ago it was clever and pointed. Now it is miserable and ambiguous.

Jesus dealt with the same thing during his ministry. So many cults of Judaism existed that the only way Jesus could separate himself from the platitudes of the day was to begin to talk about the kingdom of God. It was not only thematic, it became the headline banner for his ministry. His philosophy was: "call me a Nazarene, call me a Galilean, call me a healer, call me a kingdom teacher, call me a wine-bibber, a glutton, a friend of sinners, anything — but a Jew."

Because, as atrocious as the word *Christian* has become, the phrase *Judeo-Christian* incorporates an even greater, more insulting insipidity. There is nothing wrong with being a Jew, unless you are supposed to be a Christian. And there is nothing wrong with being a Christian, except it has lost all its external meaning. I can no longer look at the actions; or perhaps I should say, inactions — of a stumbling religious system that parades itself as Christian, and jump on the bandwagon.

The term will never be pure again.

Facts are, we have abandoned many words in our society. Prohibition. Nigger. Bull moose. League of Nations. Segregation. Manifest destiny. Indian. Slave. Midget. And "little woman."

Others that are soon to be abandoned in this humble author's opinion: the weaker sex; time-out for kids; African-American; Asian-American (or anything before American); red-neck; pro-life and pro-choice; and "ideal body weight."

Jesus said, "by your words you are justified and by your words you are condemned." I just don't feel justified anymore when I call myself a Christian. I feel condemned and cast into a pit with all the hackneyed representations of religious fervor or denominational death that reek from the pit of meaninglessness.

There is a higher calling. I want to be spiritual enough to be a practical man. Do I need a name for that? I don't know, but it sure isn't Christian. And it's not Baptist, Lutheran, Methodist, Catholic or any one of 350 other names. I do not want to become a demagogue on this issue. It is just that the word has to go.

I knew Jesus before he was a Christian. What am I supposed to do with that information? Just look at the evolution in this Christian theology of the name of Jesus. First he was Jesus of Nazareth. Then the Son of Man. Then he was Jesus Christ. Then he was Jesus Christ Our Lord. A few more years pass, and they add "Savior" to his title. Then after Savior came King of Kings followed by The Lamb of God culminating in The Coming King.

I may believe all those things about him, but they are not his name. His name is Jesus. He liked being Jesus. And through all my travels, his name is still marketable. But the word Christian can invoke anything from apathy to rage.

Jesus doesn't want to be a Christian. Dogmatic? I don't know. But since he is not here right now, I thought someone should speak up for him. Jesus does not want to hate homosexuals, even if the majority of presumed moral people feel that way. Jesus would not condone blacks and whites worshipping separately just because "they do it different." Jesus did not believe that women were supposed to be subject unto men. Jesus did not believe in children's church. He was constantly surrounded by the little tots at all times. Jesus did not begin a praise and worship team — the egos would have destroyed his ministry. Jesus did not preach against anything except the hypocrites who preached against everything. Jesus would not steal the money from widows to support his television ministry. Jesus would not start a university to foster parochial thinking and provincial scruples. Jesus would not advertise in the paper his upcoming crusade where he would be "walking on water." Jesus did not bore his audience to tears with little anecdotes and meaningless homilies leading to no change in people's lives. Jesus would not own a stained glass anything. Jesus would not allow himself to be sucked up in the political fray. Jesus would not condone a war as being "for the good of the people." Jesus would not allow women and children to be categorized as lesser citizens and objects for manipulation and control. Jesus would not be comfortable just listening to organ music. Jesus would suggest that choirs cease to sing if they must do it in a drone. Jesus would not tolerate prejudice in the guise of racial pride. Jesus would not be able to stomach theological discussion that did not lead to the relief of human conflict. Jesus would refuse all titles extolling his goodness, just like he did with the young ruler. Jesus would deflect all praise and bring focus on the faith of the people.

Jesus would chop up all the pulpits and make firewood to warm the homeless. Jesus would ask us to give more of ourselves and our hearts and less of our money and bonds.

Jesus . . . would refuse to be a Christian.

Sitting Fifteen
Jesonian

Having finished the evening's presentation, I opened the forum to questions from the audience. It was a college crowd. One very astute young man raised his hand and asked, "If you're going to take Christian away from us, what should we call ourselves?"

I know it sounds stupid, but I really hadn't pursued renaming the Christian faith, perhaps out of stupidity but mostly out of the sheer audacity of such a maneuver. I tried to sidestep the question by telling him just to focus on Jesus, his life and the power of his ministry. He wasn't satisfied. So I muttered, "Well, if they call Moses Mosaic and Paul Pauline, why can't that which is of Jesus be called, uh . . . well, Jesonian?"

There was an immediate eruption of applause. The young audience liked the word, and so did I. It is simple and easy. Stuck right in the center of it is another word — "son" — that which Jesus was to God for us, and that which we must become to our own generation, for God's sake.   Forgive me if I go ahead and phonetically spell it out here for you just to avoid confusion in pronunciation: Jah-sōn'ē-un.   It has a nice ring, doesn't it? And as far as I know, no one has ever gone to slaughter the Moors and their women and children in that name before.

Also, please forgive me for waiting until the last chapter to reveal the word, possibly breaching one of the first rules of journalism — don't bury the lead. I just thought it best to lay some groundwork and foundation if we're going to build a house of faith together.

I would like to close this book with some suggestions from this humble layman on how we might begin to address the blubbery body of Christ in its present systemized form. These are merely ideas — no better than yours, no worse than any other. Still, it is certain that we'll need to do something to free Jesus up to do what he does best, which is draw men unto himself.

At times I feel Jesus is being held hostage in a great, damp sanctuary filled with well intentioned but misguided abductors trapped in a mystical maze. Once a week they promenade him before the public and let him mumble a few words to reassure the masses that they have not harmed him and that he is still alive. Ransom is demanded in the form of tithes and offerings in order to even be granted this visitation. They are careful not to share him too much with the crowd lest his personality shine through and their diabolical cause be exposed. Yet as the weeks and months pass, interest in recovering our lost friend is waning, people not certain that such an endeavor is possible or having totally forgotten how truly wonderful he really is.

So, it has been some time since anyone has sent a rescue team in to try to retrieve him from the hands of his abductors. But I think it is time that we allow him to be free to move about as he did as a young man in Galilee, and do his own advertising and his own evangelism. So the first thing I think we have to do is:

1. **Disorganize organized religion.** I don't really care what you do — just disrupt the process that continues to produce the same product of mediocrity. Pose the question that creates the discussion that causes the teenagers in the balcony to awaken from their Sunday morning snooze. Wear the colorful garment that raises the

question of propriety. Compliment the minister when he says something other than the pre-dictable. If you're a minister, dare to leave the pulpit and take a seated position to preach to your congregation — Jesus' preference. Do something to throw sand in the gears of a machine that burns tons of energy, producing little in the way of heat. Do not deceive yourself to think that the few differences that exist within your church are enough to set you apart from the average run-of-the-mill religious factory. The slightest dribble of religiosity produces the likelihood of creating an atmos-phere of deadly hypocrisy.

Jesus did not come to establish a religion. He said, "My kingdom is not of this world. If it were, my disciples would fight." But today, the disciples do fight, which means that, somewhere along the way, we have built a man-made kingdom, which we defend. Organized religion must be disassembled — reformation will not work. We need a revolution in our thinking and a clarity in our direction. Which leads me to:

2. **We should return to our first love and promote Jesus.** The church is guilty of an Ephesian consciousness — we have lost the first love of being believers, and that is to totally be enamored by our best friend, Jesus. When I go to colleges, I have no problem talking about Jesus with students. They are intrigued and fascinated by his style, youth and smarts. But there is always some clown in the audience who wants to tie him to the Christian movement, organized religion, fundamentalism, and just general nastiness. We need to abandon the preoccupation with church doctrine causing us to tie Jesus' hands to perform only with his crucified body the act of salvation, instead of sharing his whole body, the miraculous healer and teacher. Without this return to our first love and promotion of Jesus, the general church populous will grow older and older and grayer and grayer, and more and more conservative — and afraid. For years, we have bandied about the

term "old fogey", creating a diatribe about the older folk in our churches. But the problem is not that they are old. The problem is "fogeys" of any age, who spend more time tapping the finance of the body of Christ instead of increasing the spectrum of his work. For every dollar that these "fogeys" put in the offering plate, they demand $1.20 worth of service, in décor preference and general coddling. Our old people can be trained to have dreams and our young people can catch a vision. But not as long as we insist that "fogey" opinions grounded in past traditions that have long since worn out their welcome have any relevance for this moment's ministry. I believe we can create this change best by what I refer to as:

3. **92.7–3846.** It is not a radio station, nor is it a pin number. It is the parameter of scriptures that we need to focus upon and entrust ourselves to for the time being. We have proven that, as a church, we are not competent to preach the consensus of the Bible. Too many

Old Testament singular verses and New Testament epistles taken out of context have created dissension and are often used as venom against our fellow man. We are not to be trusted with the whole Bible. It is a letter which kills because we have no spirit to give it life. I would suggest that any church or individual that would really like to become Jesonian and see true fervor in their church, should for the next two years, read, teach and preach nothing but Matthew, Mark, Luke and John through Acts 2:41. This is 92.7 chapters and 3,846 verses. If that isn't enough to keep you busy, let me know. I chose Acts 2:41 as the line in the sand where I believe the Gospel of Jesus stops and the age of the church begins. It is right after the sermon at Pentecost where 3,000 souls are added to the church and Peter has so eloquently explained the mission of Jesus and has accused the crowd of being responsible for his death. The listeners repent and are baptized and it is a glorious moment. And a glorious closing to the Jesus era. If you move to verse

42, you will find that it says: "And they continued in the apostles doctrine." This was the beginning of the age of the apostles, men's opinions, interpretations, and eventually, misguided ideas. When you do 92.7—3846 and you read these glorious words, do not ever approach them as theological jargon or inspirational fodder. They give us the heart, the breath, the soul and the sweat and blood of Jesus' thought process and mission. Whenever you read a verse, ask yourself three questions: (1) Where is he? (2) Why is he there? (3) What is really going on? You'll be astonished at your discoveries.

4. **Psalms, hymns, and spiritual songs.** Music is the greatest tool ever created to reach the hearts of men. Therefore, it is also the greatest weapon to dull the hearts of men. A great balance in our musical programs in this Jesonian fellowship is psalms, hymns and spiritual songs. Psalms are those pieces from the Bible that traditionally are used in praise and worship, understandable and warming to the human spirit.

Hymns are the songs written by our forefathers, comprehensible, filled with insight from souls who have gone on before us, who have discovered the same powerful truths that we hold dear. Spiritual songs are songs of testimony, original and written by members of our fellowship or people we know — chock-full of our language and current to our times. We miss a dimension in our worship when the talents that exist in our own group are not expressed in every service. Because music is an emotion rather than a thought or doctrine, it needs to be balanced, fresh and innovative.

5. **Pastors need to be in the marketplace.** In my thirty years of travels, I rarely met a minister who had the social skills, the business acumen and the human compassion to understand his own community. Hanging out with your congregation, raising a family, visiting in hospitals, going to movies and preaching sermons does not make for a balanced Jesonian life, one that keeps the preacher current and flexible in his thinking.

127

I don't care whether he works a part-time job (which might save the church some money) or whether he does volunteer work, or even if he has a rock band that plays on weekends in bars — anything that places him into the flow of humanity so that he can reach the Zacchaeus crowd instead of hanging out with the Nicodemus conclave. It is my great concern that if ministers do not lose their cautious preoccupation with pleasing con-gregations they will soon find themselves preaching angry words against portions of society which their members dislike and they, themselves, haven't even taken the time to know.

6. **A center for the arts.** Unless the church begins to remove all of the mahogany monstrosities of furn-iture cluttering the platforms with pretentious, wooden apparitions of intimidation we will not be able to turn the church building into a cultural center for the community to discover new concepts in music, theater and arts. If you must have pews, keep them. But take the stage and empty it of the nonsense of

wooden relics and foreboding partitions. Open your doors to the community to become the location of a wonderful auditorium to hold events. Simplify your building to make it accessible. Case in point: as powerful as it was for the church to become a center for daycare, and as successful as that project has been, it will even be more innovative to grant your auditorium as the cultural source of explosion in your town. If you want my opinion, I don't think it would hurt three or four churches to sell their buildings and move in together and develop a schedule for using the same facility with each other. You would save money and make it much clearer to the people on the outside of our movement that we were attempting to become a cohesive force instead of little islands unto ourselves.

7. **Removal of the Judeo.** We are not Jewish even though we have nothing against Judaism or its followers. Jesonian is an earthy style with an earthly message. Jesus came to fulfill and complete. When we try to blend the old with the new (in this sense, Judaism

129

with Christianity), we do exactly what he said was impossible to achieve. For he said you cannot put old wine into new wine skins. Nor can you sew new cloth onto old cloth. We wish our Jewish brothers well, but we cannot incorporate their ancient message into our burgeoning, ever-expanding philosophy. For our message is not about religious traditions or even the pursuit of God. Jesus' message was about the Kingdom of God within us, here on earth, growing and then exploring new ways to make our world more expansive. Just consider the fact that Jesus came to give us a message where God's will could be done here on earth as it is in heaven. The Old Testament, to the Jesonian believer, is great reading, but it is not life. I do not believe in being exclusive about heaven. I believe there will be Jews in heaven, Moslems, Hindus, and every religion and philosophy. I think heaven is up for grabs — firmly decided in the mind of a loving God. I think to believe anything else or to presume that from our tiny throne of insight that we can predict what happens when our hearts stop and our brains cease their streams of conscious-ness has to be the greatest manipulation of reality and spiritual genocide ever perpetuated in the history of man. I love people from all walks of life. I just don't want to dilute the Jesonian message and the power it has to transform our earthly circumstance with their opinions.

8. **Women and Children.** A Jesonian fellowship is one that rejects any notion that women are inferior and children should be seen and not heard. If we learned anything from our elder brother, Jesus, it was how to treat a lady and how to gather children unto ourselves. Jesus did not cut women any slack, expecting them to keep up, challenging any feminine wile, and ultimately asking one of them, Mary of Magdela, to be his mouthpiece to announce his resurrection to eleven men hiding in an upper room. Children live and breathe to make us question why we do things and to warn us of the dangers of pending boredom. Every religion in the world is

131

weakened by not having a total acceptance for equality of women and children. Let us not be amongst the ignorant.

9. **The Topper Ministry.** Jesus requested that we do what we can for the poor because they're not going away. We are not going to resolve the poverty question. But we become coldhearted fools if we don't address it. I think as a Jesonian person, it is our responsibility to weekly set aside for the needs of others. Amongst my friends, we do something called "The Topper" — where we take the top couple of dollars and cents of our checking accounts every week, put it in a check form, combine it together and send it off to someone or some organization in need in our community. Those $3.32 checks really add up. Just think — if 100 people in a church would do it every week, the church could be giving out $300 to $500 a week to a chosen family or organization No one ever feels the loss or notices the absence of a few dollars. My friends and myself do it over dinner and decide together where we're going

to send it. It is one of the high points of our week and truly one of those glorious, warm and fuzzy experiences in our spiritual journey.

10. Let morality work itself out. I find when I have my nose in other people's business, it is hard for me to breathe. And I want to breathe. I want to live and let live. No one has ever dropped a vice because I demanded, requested or even suggested that they do. It's just the nature of things. We are a jealous people who change because we want what other people have. If you want to improve the morality of your planet, stop preaching morality and start living contentment and success. Jesus' disciples wanted to rain fire and lightening down from heaven onto people. He told them they did not know what spirit was at work in them. Good point. Same for us, Jesus. We need to leave people alone. We are not going to change them. We cannot stop sin by shining a light on it. We should have learned that by now. Prohibition does not prohibit anything, it just makes it clandestine and sneaky. So here's an idea — love your neighbor as yourself. If you don't want anybody in your business — stay out of theirs. And by the way, mine too. I often tell people, if they want to dig up dirt on me, take a small shovel and they won't even need to pack a lunch. Like everyone else, I make enough mistakes to prove my humanity. Do yourself the greatest favor. Put your hand to the plow and don't turn back.

Jesonian: a decision to make Jesus, and Jesus only, the center of our earthly odyssey. We reject all gods of doctrine, all legalism that alienates us from loving our fellowman, and all practice that lacks practicality. Instead, we embrace the one who told us that his ways are easy and his burden is light. *Jesonian* — a determination to cease to be religious and dare to be real, first to ourselves and then to our fellow man.

The End

Jonathan Richard Cring

Jonathan Richard Cring is the composer of fourteen symphonies, the author of eleven books, including **I'M . . . the legend of the son of man, Liary, Holy Peace . . .the story of Iz and Pal, Jesonian, Finding the Lily, Digging for Gold and 20 other reasons to kiss a frog.** His thirty-year experience has taken him from the grease paint of theater to a time as an evangelist among the gospel saints. He is the winner of a Billboard Music Award and is the in-house composer for the Sumner County Symphony. He travels the country lecturing as an advocate for the Jesonian movement. He has been married for thirty-five years and is the father of three sons and guardian to three others. He lives in Hendersonville, Tennessee.

Also from the Author

All books available through Amazon.com and
WWW.LWSBOOKS.COM

Living a Legendary Life
ISBN 978-1-5997562-2-6

Jonathan Richard Cring has penned a new book for every
person weary of chasing the lottery and waiting for dreams to
come true. Living a Legendary Life is a call to arms to begin to
take what we know and apply it to where we are, molding it into
why we believe. A thought from the book: "Someone needs to sit
down and tell every man, woman and child, 'Hey! You're not going
to be famous--but you can be legendary.'" A legendary life. A
decision to take our life and stay alert and practical, as if it were
the only life we will ever have. For after all, it is.

20 other reasons to kiss a frog
ISBN 978-0-9704361-4-6

Leaping into the mainstream of social consciousness and
human interactions, Jonathan Richard Cring offers his new nonfiction volume 20 OTHER REASONS TO KISS A FROG, a look
at today's life with parallels and insight from our friend in the

pond. Featuring titles like: THEY TREAT ALL WOMEN LIKE PRINCESSES, THEY KEEP THEIR TONGUES TO THEMSELVES and THEY ARE NOT ASHAMED OF THEIR TADPOLE YEARS the fast-paced sittings offer comedy and insight--a human blending of delight.

Jesonian
A decision to take spirituality personally.
ISBN 978-0-9704361-4-6

Stagnancy is the decision to settle for less than we know we need. In every generation there must be a voice reminding us of our true mission, prodding us on to escape mediocrity and stirring the waters to freshen the stream of thinking. Jesonian is a book that poses the questions in the heart of every human who seeks to find some nourishment for his hardening soul – every man, woman and child who yearns for a message with meaning and wants to escape the rigors of religion and find the true spirit in spirituality.

Finding the Lily (to consider)
A journette of the journey.
ISBN 978-0-9704361-5-3

All books available through Amazon.com and
WWW.LWSBOOKS.COM

When I was a kid, they didn't have Big Men's Stores - at least, none my parents told me about. So my mother would buy me the only pants she could find in my size - work pants.

Dickie work pants. For some reason, she would choose the green ones - the color created by smashing a bag of green peas into a frog. And speaking of being smashed, for some reason, she wouldn't buy them my size, I guess because she didn't want to admit how big I was. And so she would purchase them so small that I would have to suck in to button them. That's what you like when you're fat. Tight green clothes. Of course, these pants were so stiff they could stand by themselves, which I have to admit, came in handy when waiting in line at an amusement park.

Digging for Gold [in the rule]
ISBN 978-0-9704361-6-0

The Golden Rule, Do unto others as you would have them do unto you, loses some of its gleam and luster when merely decoupaged and hung on a wall in a Sunday School class as some sort of insipid platitude, more an aspiration than a lifestyle.

In DIGGING FOR GOLD (in the rule), author Cring examines the intricacies and passion of the original thought and also offers innovative approaches to turning the "Rule" into a reality.

Chocked full of stories, examples and plans of action, DIGGING is a must for the soul who desires to have their spirituality flowing in the mainstream instead of entombed in the sanctuary of religious redundancy.

All books available through Amazon.com and
WWW.LWSBOOKS.COM

Holy Peace . . . the story of Iz and Pal
ISBN 978-0-9704361-3-9

In a basket full of oranges, it is always the singular apple that gains our attention. This is a wonderful characteristic of the human soul. So in our day and age, in the midst of clamoring for resolutions based on military might, a breath of fresh air comes in to the atmosphere of pending war. Amir and Jubal – two boys who grew up on different sides of the tracks of a conflict – one Arab, one Jew. They rename themselves Iz and Pal and determine to maintain their friendship amidst the granite – headed thinking of their friendship amidst the granite-headed thinking of their society. Where their journey takes them, the friends they make along the way, the surprising enemies, and the stunning resolution, will keep you riveted to the brief pages of this odyssey into peace.

by Jonathan

I'M . . .
the legend of the son of man
ISBN 978-0-9704361-3-9

A novel on the life of Jesus Christ focusing on his humanity, passion, and personality—highlighting struggles with his family, sexuality, abduction by zealots,

All books available through Amazon.com and
WWW.LWSBOOKS.COM

humor and wit, and interaction with characters bound by tradition, affection, legalism, politics, and religious fanaticism—congealed into a 416 page entertaining and inspirational quick read; non-theological and mind enriching.

Preparing a Place [for myself]
ISBN 978-0-9704361-7-7

The perfect book for all those folks who would like to die just long enough to find out what the crap is going on – then come back to pizza. I always wanted to meet God. When I was a child, very small, I thought he would look like Reverend Bacorra, a Presbyterian minister I knew- salt and pepper hair, tall, glasses, donning a black robe, wearing oxblood, shiny shoes with scuffed tips.

As I grew older my image changed, but always, I envisioned a physical presence – an actual being. Now, where was God?

I wondered if God was merely light, love and spirit. I smiled at my own ramblings. Light, love and spirit - not a bad triangle.

Still, I wanted to meet God, fact to face, as it were.
a bad triangle.
Still, I wanted to meet God, fact to face, as it were.

NOTES

NOTES

CPSIA information can be obtained at www.ICGtesting.com
Printed in the USA
LVOW070516120313

323792LV00001B/2/A